How can I improve my day...?

Exploring diverse perspectives and responses to take a step to a more fulfilling life

By
George Cimpoeru

MAPLE
PUBLISHERS

How can I improve my day...?

Author: George Cimpoeru

Copyright © 2026 George Cimpoeru

The author asserts the moral right to be identified as the author of this work.

The right of George Cimpoeru to be identified as author of this work has been asserted by the author in accordance with section 77 and 78 of the Copyright, Designs and Patents Act 1988.

First Published in 2026

ISBN 978-1-83538-530-2 (Paperback)
    978-1-83538-881-5 (Hardback)
    978-1-83538-531-9 (E-book)

Book Cover Design and Book Layout by:
    White Magic Studios
    www.whitemagicstudios.co.uk

Published by:
    Maple Publishers
    Fairbourne Drive, Atterbury,
    Milton Keynes,
    MK10 9RG, UK
    www.maplepublishers.com

A CIP catalogue record for this title is available from the British Library.

All rights reserved. No part of this book may be reproduced or translated in any form or by any means, electronic or mechanical, including photocopying, recording or by any information storage and retrieval system without written permission from the author.

The views expressed in this work are solely those of the author and do not reflect the opinions of Publishers, and the Publisher hereby disclaims any responsibility for them. This book should not be used as a substitute for the advice of a competent authority, admitted or authorized to advise on the subjects covered.

Contents

- Lessons and Acknowledgments 4
- Introduction 10
- Happiness, the premium desire... 14
- Going through difficult times 55
- The battle of conflictual beliefs 79
- Emotional equilibrium - the golden ratio............................. 90
- The error of confirmation 110
- Perception vs actual experience 117
- A false sense of confidence 125
- Human performance & effectiveness 129
- Fundamental attribution error 152
- Perfect fairness, the irrational expectation 158
- Vivid and unreliable memories 165
- The role of luck and its probability 170
- The unknown unknown 182
- The ability to unlearn 187
- Improving the day… 191
- Preferring a nice lie over the difficult truth… 208
- The inversion approach 213
- Hope, nothing without it… 217
- References 219

Lessons and Acknowledgments

Every person we meet in our lives comes with a lesson or a reason. If it's in a good way, we try to remember them, if it's in a bad way we probably remember them even more. Neutrality plays its role too, not everything has to have a reason behind and that itself represents one. Whenever we encounter such scenarios, it gives a chance to reflect on ourselves and not only what truly matters at the time, but in the long term too. More importantly, it gives us an opportunity to become more aware within certain events and to improve our behaviour if needed.

Over the years, my father has often given me the idea how to find joy over the little things in life. I have learned not to complain when it comes to emotional and physical pain even in the presence of difficult moments. He did not participate in deceitful and violent acts, nor being dishonest to himself or to the family. Along the way, I was exposed to different approaches to improve both personal development and to become better as a person. Helping someone in need was one of them. Unfortunately, he passed away in July 2024 at the age of fifty-eight. I would like to dedicate this book to his memory.

From my mother, I have witnessed how a moral obligation and responsibility towards herself and towards family played its part throughout her 38 years of marriage. She often reminded herself to treat her daily life with compassion, regardless of any circumstantial factors. Her ambitious mindset kept her motivated in a given context, especially when it comes to a family reason. Key aspects such as devotion and commitment were also not missing, to support the long-term marriage and how to become more adaptable to different life experiences.

From my brother, always to support and love whenever a situation requires to do so.

From Vasilica, choosing kindness with no hesitation, sharing and offering something from the heart, without asking too many questions and any other expectations, negotiations or limitations.

From my former boss Olaf Göbel, I have learned how to be more rational with ourselves and with those around, visualising "the things" for what they are, in a clear manner, not to mention there is never a good time either to start something off or to finish it. He continuously aimed to lead by example, where vision and trust were predominantly used, challenging his team to improve and to further expand their professional experience. He was not in favour of chauffeur knowledge, often expressing himself with moral characteristics and idioms, not taking credit for his own performance and neither for someone within the team, "There is a lot of rubbish behind the door that we don't see!"

In the first days of studies, I met Sina. After the first class, an assignment was handed over to us. We met randomly in the library. Since we shared the same module, he asked how I was finding a particular question due to its higher complexity. He offered his help regarding that task. It was nice of him to do so. Since the subject of the project was, I thought at the time within my circle of competence, I said no, as I was almost undoubtful in that specific problem-solving approach. We exchanged the two methodologies within the assignment, just to see a different perspective. "There is only one way to find out," I said. After some time, we got the results. I couldn't be more wrong! We have kept in touch ever since. Gradually, I have learned never giving up on one's dreams and personal goals regardless of the timeframe and progress, not for oneself but for the people whom one loves the most. Mostly everything with a touch of humour and humbleness in doing so.

From Ross Hodgkinson, I valued the practising of self-care in a friendly manner, in every aspect of life such as personal well-being, life satisfaction or even in times of adversity.

From Alexander, how to continuously seek to maximise professional development in a given time. Promoting and aiming for a work-life balance to switch between the two, was another characteristic.

Sebastian Ludwig has given me the impression of what it looks like to hold a passion for engineering in order to analyse, share and master his innovative skills.

From Dr Rachel, I have learned what a supportive person should look like when a situation most needs one, constantly attracting the flavour of sympathy with good intentions and innate abilities to match her individual personality with professional experience.

From Jim Kwik, I understood how the biggest weakness can become the greatest strength over time, and ultimately making a difference in the world by actively sharing in the learning and development experience.

Kojo Numah proposed that placing one's trust in diverse working conditions can increase both productivity and collaboration.

From Susan David, not only how to show up to our own emotions: with gentle acceptance, love, curiosity, but also how to become more agile with ourselves based on what we experience at the time.

From myself, I have learned how small improvements or setbacks can significantly impact our journey, for better or worse. These effects can diversify from any aspect of wellbeing, knowledge or prosperity of any kind. Doing something no matter how small towards a healthier diet, a healthier decision or even a lifestyle. In case of prosperity, delaying actions or leaving something to the last minute can often result in more issues that can be easily avoidable. Those can create much more unprecedented scenarios and eventually their subsequent consequences. One of the core contributions to a self-improvement approach is to recognise our own patterns of thoughts, feelings and what we do on a regular basis. In other words, identifying our own flaws, tendencies and preconceptions of how we see ourselves and the world we live in. At the end, taking an action towards any progress that can be made. During different experiences, I understood how varied thinking styles can sometimes play tricks with us, leading to flawed reasoning approaches at the time, affecting both our decision-making process and behaviour. Furthermore, holding a holistic approach makes us more aware of our own behaviour when it comes to physical, emotional and spiritual wellbeing. I would call it the 'triangle', which significantly impacts every aspect of life. When one side is altered, it has consequences on the other two sides and vice versa. The triangle's silhouette continuously changes as we go along.

Abstract

We all experience difficulties and different challenges throughout life. They are inevitable. Some people to a greater extent than others. As a result, we develop various thinking styles and coping strategies to deal with such events. At the same time, we are continuously striving to be better and ultimately happier. This is all what we want eventually, at the beginning, at the end and as we go along. This book highlights various insights to become more aware of what makes us happy and in contrast, what makes us unhappy. It also identifies the process when facing something difficult, what can be accomplished and not, as well as the underlying stages when something is performed effectively through trial and failure. Some of the unhelpful thinking approaches we are exposed to, and some of the good ones too, are not excluded in this book such as the attribution error, the role of luck with or without merit through a normalised method and even dealing with the unexpected from time to time.

Whenever we encounter these scenarios, one of the valuable approaches throughout is self-awareness. Simply, to understand what we are going through and to distinguish between different alternatives that might be available to us at the time. A difficult situation doesn't necessarily mean pain, discomfort, vulnerability. It can also translate into prosperity, learning, contentment, gratefulness and resilience. Similarly, in the case of happiness: comfort, relaxation, high levels of excitement and optimism can provide unhappiness, disappointment, anxiousness and fragility. Both concepts are part of life. They continuously harmonise and work hand in hand. When you smell something nice, for example flowers, you tend to value more the same smell if you previously had to smell an unpleasant one. It creates a contrast that amplifies in the opposite direction. The same smell is intensified and would not have the same effect without the unpleasant one. Nothing's changed, it's the same scent from the beginning.

Of course, just becoming aware of a situation, doesn't bring effectiveness or problem-solving skills, we still need to test it against the reality we live in. This is because the concept within our inner world is often different from the one we face in real time. With that in mind, we are more likely to act in a specific manner, the way we think and feel before showing up to certain situations. Our behaviour is often displayed as a by-product of the inner senses (emotions, thoughts, feelings, memories), representing a side effect. The end outcome still remains uncertain. During a situation, those senses amongst other exposing factors can change the anticipated decisions and behaviour. Eventually, those will display an improvement in our daily life. Self-awareness increases the chances of being more in line with the reality we live in, for a more authentic and prosperous life.

Introduction

In the year 2020, I experienced several changes. Those changes varied from a breakup, covid-19 breakout, a substantial financial loss to a change in residence a few times in less than a year. Job satisfaction wasn't great either. Some of the setbacks occurred simultaneously in a short period of time. These fluctuations amongst a few others, had brought me a high volatility in terms of emotional context. The emotions and thoughts aroused with those changes were extremely profound. Something was happening and I didn't know what it was, experiencing them for the first time in that sort of intensity. Once I was going through those changes, I started to write down my thoughts, feelings, and any potential plans where applicable. Ever since I remember, I had an inclination for writing things down, especially actions and plans. This time was different, it wasn't in a productive way. Most of them were with a gloomy outlook, rather than in a realistic way. As time went by, I began to fill dozens of pages with writings, mainly with what I was experiencing at the time. It was a combination of thoughts, feelings, plans in relation to the past, present and future. Therefore, I started to look to a deeper context behind those, often questioning myself: Are they normal? Why is this happening? What can be done in this context? Most emotions at that time were invariably intense. They were difficult, painful, unexpected, confounded for longer than usual. The architecture of my own belief system was unclear, ambiguous, contradictory. As a result, I began to emphasise more about those emotions and thoughts. To a great extent, as I was researching and writing about them,

I asked myself in contrast: I am experiencing those moments and feelings and not in the healthiest way... But what makes me happy as a human being? How can I improve my day? At the time and up to that point I had this view on life, which I considered may lead towards happiness. Nothing out of the ordinary, probably like most people in their time frame: good health as individuals and towards family, job satisfaction, a healthy relationship, living a comfortable life financially, the presence of feel-good moments, travelling more, doing more of one's own interests amongst few others. As a self-explanatory concept now, there was a lot more than I imagined behind the word 'happiness'. This is all what we want eventually. In other words, to be happy, satisfied and make the most of life. Not long after, I had these 2 concepts in mind, a state of melancholy and happiness. I wanted to integrate something additionally that I believed was important at the time, some of the common thinking errors that we might all encounter and some of the good ones too that are used in a sustainable way to grow and improve.

I am George Cimpoeru, 34 years old. I was born in a normal working family. My parents tried their best to provide for us well, which I am proud of. I was one of the younger siblings. Sometimes, no matter how much they tried, there was still not enough to ensure something was not missing. This has made me more determined to follow whichever path I was going to follow. Since an early age, I had a tendency of working with numbers. When the time arrived at the crossroads, to make an educational decision, I chose the field of engineering. This was to combine the analytical skills within a real application. The automotive field was a hot industry at the time. The sector had been growing continuously in number, scope and complexity especially on the development part and environmental sustainability. Working in the engineering background for approximately 8 years, I wanted to draw attention in this sector too. This has given me a good understanding how things are created, developed and sustained throughout time in relation to people's needs. Thus, I emphasised on the concept of human performance, how this is achieved and the underlying stages towards the effectiveness of such performance. For instance, how the automobile industry began, and developed through the years. In addition, how something is effectively performed and maintained can vary through different stimuli, challenges, and neural state oscillations experienced throughout the day, shifting from one to another. It doesn't happen instantly; it takes a long time until the best of the best is achieved. During the writing of this book, I have experienced many sorts of emotional states. These states covered a broad spectrum of feelings, from neglectfulness, omission, enthusiasm, abandonment, sluggishness, creativity, productivity, postponement, motivation, inspiration and the list continues. My natural curiosity pulled me along the way to finish what I started. The intense feelings I had, have led me to write about those, not because I was in a comfort and relaxation mode. In opposition, these were much needed working as a recovery function to start again and prepare for the next challenges. When I go back in time – metaphorically, I can notice the difference between different experiences and emotional states. Before an event, we think we know what we should do in a particular case, but often do not know how to step out of those situations, especially when something happens for the first time. One of the fundamental human pre-dispositions that I was exposed to, distorted my thinking to believe otherwise. With that in mind, there are no permanent states of sadness or happiness as we go along, as emotional states, motivations and priorities change, subside, intensify, disappear or return. One moment we feel one way, next we feel another way. Fluctuating moods happen all the time depending on what we do, what we think, and what we're exposed to. As a note, I never had the intention of writing a book for an audience. It was something for my own purpose, as a requisite for self-guiding approach. After some time, my perception was adjusted. I believe some people may encounter some of these concepts and perhaps find this book useful in the learning and sharing experience.

I
Happiness, the premium desire

What are we truly after as a human being? Perhaps, one of the million-dollar questions!

Today's era represents the best time to be alive in recorded history. We've got internet - where we can connect with someone from miles away, faster commuting ways like never before, opportunities of any kind, medical support, human rights, the privilege of choice and yet we are not as happy as we wish to be. At the same time, people are more fragile and exposed to unhappiness than ever. According to research and happiness index report, we were happier a few centuries ago than now. Why ...? People focused on different things such as health and life expectancy, when comparing them to today's measures of happiness.

There are numerous reasons and activities that increase the level of happiness. Above all, what is happiness and how can it be measured? Well, happiness means different things to different people. It can be diversified from the inner self to wellbeing, wealth, family, love, personal growth or the quality of life. The list continues further to professional career, success, autonomy, status, and so on. To start with, one of the key factors is to 'allow' us to be happy, starting from our internal thoughts and emotions. Mostly everything happens in our mind, how we perceive the world, what surrounds us, and what we embrace. When taking a closer look, almost anything can become examples of attraction, pleasure or just beauty on its own. Simply, observing the Mother

Nature, closely or loosely into the far horizon, represents one of them. This can be further accompanied by tasting the *'richness'* of life. To be able to see, move, touch, breathe and translate the world we live in. We can also start with the moments we are exposed to the most in our daily routine. Things or moments that are used at a high frequency such as eating, cooking, occupation, dressing, leisure, or the people we spend time with. In other terms, things that are 'simple', common and necessary, regardless of any imaginary attributions we may possess such as wealth, the place in the social hierarchy, or financial status. That's because we have a much higher chance to make the most of them due to their high usage.

Shortly after, we can observe the things that are also unpleasant or less beautiful. These notions are varied from a flight cancellation in the last minute, working with someone we don't like, or a closed family member having to check into the local hospital. When it comes to our own conduct, if someone displays an inappropriate behaviour or becomes violent, yet they can also be kind and friendly at the same time, something tragic may have happened in their lives, they could be in danger or in need of help. Witnessing this, we tend to realise that we are not exempt from flaws and things are not that good as we think when paying closer attention to ourselves. Who hasn't said something wrong and thereafter felt sorry? Or who hasn't broken their promise? This is what makes us different, unique in our own way. Our ideas, thinking, feelings and behaviour are a reflection of everything that happens in our lives whether it is an outside or internal state. Once we become more aware of those senses, having a wider perspective within ourselves and what is around us, we can then become our own author of the premium desire.

There is not a fluid definition of happiness. It's a multi-dimensional concept that comes in many ways, forms and shapes while it keeps evolving. Whatever made us happy 5 or 10 years ago, the same thing doesn't anymore. Happiness can be described as an emotional reaction to an outcome, a result supported by a set of conditions. If I get that promotion - I will be happy, if I engage in that relationship - I will be happy. Similarly, when I get a new car, a house, finish that project, achieve financial freedom, retirement and so on. Mostly, everything is saved for later. This is often described as a delayed happiness. These preliminary conditions are regarded sensible and reasonable ways, describing good incentives to look forward to such scenarios. They represent a sense of 'safety', a sense of 'freedom' for the individual. Moreover, these conditions lead further to postponements, for example, "I will do more of x when I get y", expecting that you will become closer to the person you want to be when y happens. However, those delays and any of their kind can lead to consequences and associated risks. On one hand, it may not happen; on the other we look for an extra thing that becomes our next focus of attention, but more importantly, whenever the result dependent will take place, the way we come up to any of those moments will no longer serve us, because we are a different person, a new self, both cognitively and physically. Perhaps showing signs of a medical condition or the energy is no longer at the preferred levels.

In addition, happiness can be triggered by anticipation, memories or moments. Imagining something nice, feels good and pleasant, imagining something worrying or troubling, feels uncomfortable, painful. In terms of moments, moments that are created by us or by external factors, happiness is eventually a side effect of those moments, which normally doesn't last long. Whenever we experience something enjoyable, shortly afterwards our happiness starts to dissipate, going back to the original state or worse. Happiness can also be defined as the overall satisfaction in the course of an individual's life. Another way to describe happiness is through the experience of pleasant and positive feelings. Or simply as the psychologist Nobel prize winner Daniel Kahneman defines it: "What I experience here and now!"

As a society, according to the World Happiness Report in 2023, Finland and Denmark are ranked as the top countries in the world when it comes to happiness. This is based on the 6-item measure of life satisfaction. These measures consist of emotional and physical wellbeing, social and financial status, career and community support. These two countries are not the richest in terms of GDP per capita, nor having luxurious skyscrapers or weather conditions, but instead they tend to believe that work-life balance is the superior factor. Another contributing factor to their happiness is that most people in these countries are in the middle class on the financial sector. This is a good indicator as the majority don't have to confront the extreme scale of unequal opportunity. From generous parental leave, free education and healthcare to a government and trust community, all are considered under the work-life balance. Furthermore, working a weekly average of 36 hours, will allow the individuals to do more in their free time, or spend it with their loved ones.

Let's explore different aspects and reasons that boost the level of human happiness and lead towards it. According to Abraham Maslow, there are 5 human needs that drive the motivation of our behaviour in life. This is called Maslow's pyramid of human needs. Abraham Maslow was an American psychologist, and in 1943 developed this idea in a paper entitled 'A Theory of Human Motivation', considered one of the core foundations of psychological and behavioural sciences in modern history. His work was emphasised on what we are looking for as a human being and what naturally are our intentions. These 5 human needs are represented in a hierarchy and once we reach a certain level, we plan and intend to move to the next one, becoming our next focus of attention.

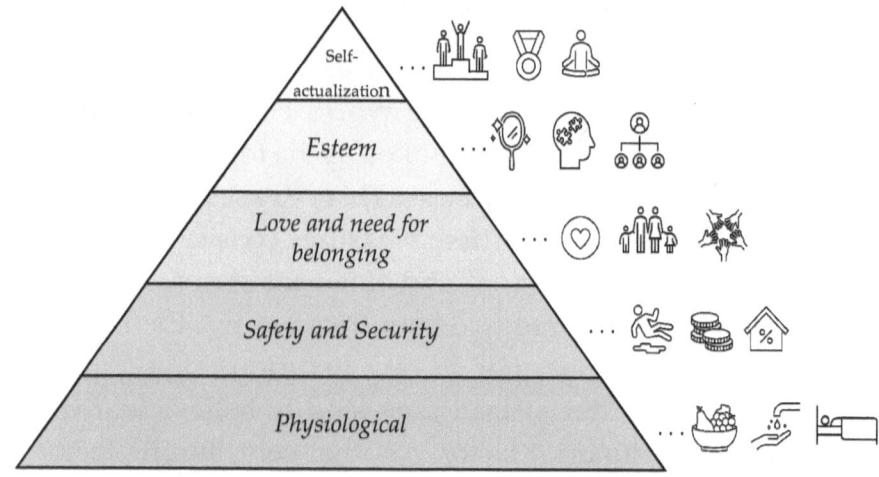

Maslow's Pyramid of Human Needs

1. **Physiological.** These are the most important needs, and they are non-negotiable such as water, food, oxygen, temperature, sleep. These needs are essential to human survival. They are also needed to fulfil the anatomy's requirement for homeostasis. They are designed to maintain regular levels and dynamic equilibrium of body temperature, heart beating rate, blood pressure and so on. When an individual is missing more than one need, the physiological needs become their first focus of interest. For example, when a person is significantly thirsty or freezing due to low temperature, it's extremely difficult to concentrate or to pay attention to anything else. Certainly, we do not look to improve our grammar skills or Spanish, but alternatively seeking for water or a warmer place. You may wonder, how does this need, or any other need reflect on happiness? Surely, it has an impact on happiness, for instance if you didn't eat the whole day or didn't go to

sleep for 2 days consecutively due to unspecified reasons and, once you have a rich meal or good night's sleep, you will feel different after, which consequently leads to a happier state. As a result, the happiness level raises with each level of needs.

2. **Safety and Security.** Now, after the first level, the individual has the strongest desire to feel safe and secure. In this section, physical and emotional health are included as well as a safe environment, financial safety, violence protection, free from natural disasters and any other threat to life or dangerous conditions. A steady income, knowing our loved ones are safe, accessing a health service and insurance, including a property to call 'home', are all covered in this sector. The first two levels are called the basic needs or deficiency needs.

3. **Love and need for belonging.** This stage includes love expressed not only romantically, but also towards friends, family, and others. Additionally, the need to feel attached that we are part of something, experiencing affection towards someone, feeling loved and accepted by our peers, society, or work environment. Trust, intimacy, and sympathy play their role too in this phase.

4. **Esteem.** These needs are categorised in two types: lower esteem, referred as external validation and higher esteem, identified as internal self-worth. Lower esteem covers success, appreciation, respect, recognition, job title, status. Under higher esteem is included self-respect, personal worth, confidence, knowledge and competence. In this context, these needs involve the individuals to feel good about themselves, valuable and important, particularly when their achievements are recognised by the society. Wealth, luxurious lifestyle, and physical appearance are all representing a contribution of it. Levels 3 and 4 of

Maslow's hierarchy are referred to psychological needs. When esteem needs are low or absent, individuals may experience feelings of inferiority.

5. **Self-actualisation.** At the top of the pyramid level, an individual desires to reach the full potential as a human being. This self-actualisation is normally unique or different to each of us. For example, the individual wants to be the best in a certain domain, wishes to be a role model, the wealthiest, widest, greatest parent, the top artist, educator, musician, athlete and the list continues. All personal and world records are achieved in this level. Normally, these needs are extremely rare and difficult to achieve. In addition, most of the wonderful and interesting events occur in this phase, but they do not always align with individual's intentions. Jaqueline Way, a mother of 3 children, inspired the world with the project called 365give. The idea behind 365give was to create an act of kindness every single day of the year. She initially started to teach her little son of 3, then later passed this remarkable project through the local school, community, and society. She later became the co-founder of the 365 give platform.

With the aim to reduce human suffering, Alan Watkins offers another example of a self-actualisation form. Working for more than 12 years as physician and neuroscientist, he wanted to have a greater impact when it comes to people's suffering. He thought that helping someone on an individual basis is not enough. By founding his own company 'Complete Coherence' in 2004, Alan believed to do so, the best way is to start from the top to bottom in the professional or social hierarchy. After a decade, he teaches leaders from the world's largest companies to become more effective and ultimately take better decisions in both personally or professionally. He focuses on the development and the effectiveness within the decision-making processes, how those affect different key metrics and ultimately people's lives.

Every single day we are exposed to, comes with the pyramid of human needs. Constantly alternating from one to another. When it comes to the last needs, they are constantly developing as we go along, for example the desire we have had few years, or months ago, might not motivate us now. Over the years, Maslow's pyramid of needs was updated to some degree. Additional needs were added to better reflect the complexity of human motivation The order outline doesn't have to be strictly followed too, especially in the final needs, since the self-actualization phase cannot be verified precisely. There could be a substantial discussion about love, financial status, or profession, which alternates between 3 and 4, where they overlap. For some people achieving 'status' level 4 might be more important than attaining love, level 3. Also, the pyramid takes no account of cultural and social background where people may consider and perceive a need in a distinctive way. People in less developed countries show a sensitive way of happiness, despite not having access to a 'comfortable' life, while exposed to different challenges compared to the general population. Providing food as a basic necessity while sharing it with their families represents one reason. Other factors include the limitations within the close vicinity or reduced number of options.

Maslow believed there were various circumstances or requirements which are not mentioned on the pyramid, as the people progress through the hierarchy of needs. For example, expressing freely or living in a fair community. Additionally, he highlighted that developing new ideas and learning new things to comprehend the reality or society around us can be defined as essential needs. One reason is that we feel safer which contributes to our self-fulfilment needs. Usually, most individuals have their first 3-4 levels of needs partially met. One activity can satisfy more than two needs simultaneously. For example, working as a nurse can provide the wages for someone to pay for food and accommodation and at the same time can offer a sense of satisfaction and social interaction. Monetary value can influence every stage of the pyramid of human needs. It's a way of measuring happiness offering people a sense of security, a sense of freedom to be able to do more with their free time or simply exchanging the cost of physiological needs.

As an individual, you may ask yourself what comes next after reaching the top of the pyramid. For example, what are you after once you become the best of what you do or what you wished for. There are a few things an individual may contend with:

- The individual tends to desire consistency, wanting to remain in that particular state, whether it's wealth, fame, profession or similar aspects. They aim to stay at the top of hierarchy for as long as possible.
- The person may be subjected to the fear of losing 'everything' out. This emotion can become way too intense, leading them to constantly find different solutions or alternatives to avoid such a scenario.
- Limited time is a universal challenge we all face, regardless of any circumstantial factors, where a person wants to stop the time, wishing to go back in time, or create more.

Happiness is also grounded on short and long-term contexts. Happiness is experienced differently across age groups. For example, short-term happiness includes boosting your energy, pleasure or positive that can be felt on the moment, on the day, often derived from exploring or trying new things. In contrast, long-term happiness is more about life satisfaction, how an individual views their life in the present or future. Moreover, when considering the age scale, when you are in your 20's you will find happiness in another way compared to someone in their 60's, largely due to different life experiences that are encountered between the two.

Genetic influence. According to research, around 40% when it comes to happiness is due to the genetic factors. This is a substantial portion considering the inherited traits, DNA or personality influencing factors contribute as much. Some people are exposed even to a higher degree on this spectrum. Before we are born, we already start the life journey between approximately -40 or +40 before we do anything else. The remaining percentage is subjected to the individual, personal experiences, lifestyle, environment and other exposures. The core characteristics from a person's DNA provides a blueprint from predecessors which are passed down together with personality traits amongst other features. If the extreme scale is considered, the difference doubles between 2 persons. An individual with an unhappier genetic background will be subjected to a lot more effort than others to reach the premium desire. However, when it happens, the happiness will 'taste' better in return. The genetic background will remind us from time to time of our own inheritance. Over the years, I have encountered people who naturally exhibit this characteristic, regardless of any circumstantial factors they may experience at the time, including difficult challenges, health conditions, or other life exposures.

'Feeling alive' moments. Numerous studies indicate that the release of adrenaline can be added as a contributing factor to the individual's happiness. This is when the body and mind get ready before facing an extreme situation. The heart beats faster, blood pressure goes up, the brain is in a high alert mode, while the body temperature starts to increase. Whether it's excitement, fear or a fine line between the two, this happens during an extreme sport experience, facing a danger or a situation with a strong emotional impact. For example, driving a car at an extremely high speed, engaging in extreme sports such as skydiving, mountain climbing, zip-wiring, or perhaps taking a financial decision with high volatility in the market.

To further extend the word happiness, there are four happy hormones performing like regulators or transmitters within our bodily system. These hormones are chemical reactions created by various glands that help stimulate or regulate the level of pleasure, satisfaction, mood, or happiness. Each hormone activates in a specific way based on the emotions and feelings an individual experiences in response to different circumstantial situations.

Dopamine. Often called the 'feeling good' hormone, its main function is to trigger pleasure and reward. In other terms, the neurotransmitter that expresses, "This feels good, I want more...!" There are certain situations or activities that contribute towards this level of dopamine. For example, imagine walking into your friend's house and start smelling cakes in the oven. It feels great, doesn't it? Other examples of activities that release this hormone include celebrating a win, during a shopping activity, listening to your favourite music or experiencing arousal during intimate moments. You have been studying hard for the last year, as soon as the exams finishes, pfft...! it brings such a big relief. Similarly, when planning an event such as a wedding day or the college graduation. Ticking something off your to-do list, solving a problem, doing something new and creative also play a substantial part within the brain reward system. When an individual has something on his mind, e.g. an action plan and all the tasks are completed accordingly within a time limit, it also activates this hormone. In other words, creating a feeling of productivity and effectiveness. Another example of a reward is when posting on a social media platform where the 'like' button is reacted with any additional comments, remarks, or agreements. Furthermore, when a game is played with multiple levels, progressing to the next level while guided by the new incentives. The dopamine hormone can be triggered as a reward when someone breaks the law, does something immoral, and gets away with it. Some people call this activity as the dopamine rush. The moderate usage of alcohol and drugs is not disregarded acting as a boost in the dopamine level offering a short-term effect of 'euphoria'. However, these transient moments can lead to a false sense of confidence and self-perception. An increase level of those catalysts can negatively impact both, the emotional and physical wellbeing of an individual. Those catalysators can be extremely addictive, making the individual to want more and can cause harm over time.

Serotonin. This hormone aims to control and regulate the individual's mood. Known as the mood stabiliser, it helps and promotes the feelings of satisfaction, relaxation, and wellbeing. Furthermore, it's designed to adjust the individual's digestive system, desire for appetite, sleeping pattern, or some of the cognitive functions including memory and learning abilities. There are various activities that can improve a person's mood and their disposition. This hormone is activated whenever we are exposed to sunlight, engage in regular exercise throughout the day or maintain a balanced diet. Additionally, 'simple measures' such as going for a walk in the nature, listening to the birds' songs and noise of sea waves, or admiring what the wonderful world may offer at that time, are few other examples. Low levels of serotonin can cause discomfort and affect emotional wellbeing, while high levels of serotonin can cause agitation, distress and anxiety.

Oxytocin. Known as the 'love hormone', this is mainly activated during childbirth, love or any physical and romantic affection. Its role is to encourage a strong interaction in parent-child relationships and any other. Engaging in activities such as giving compliments, playing with a baby or pet, and helping others can significantly increase the levels of this hormone.

Endorphins. This group of hormone is normally generated to overcome the level of tension and discomfort while improving the individual's mood. Laughing, singing, dancing, exercising or simply eating rich foods including chocolate, are only few activities that promotes the release of this hormone.

Chasing the **'previous best experience'**. Many of our days we remember is when something good or bad happened. Something wonderful or tragic. Most of the other days are lost in routine. The 'previous best experience' involves when we experience something with a high emotional impact when it comes to remembering. More specifically, it highlights the most intense point related to those memories. You probably heard the following sentence: 'I remember like it was yesterday.' Clearly wasn't yesterday, it was 15 years ago! The emotional event is simply a shortcut to our memories when we recall how we felt in the transient moment rather than the whole experience. Therefore, we evaluate an event or experience based only on 'few fragments of reality'. Any other moments prior or after the peak we tend to miss, where less important aspects of an experience occur. This applies for both, pleasant and unpleasant moments. When it comes to happiness, we want to remember the outcomes that yield the most favourable results. Therefore, thinking about how we felt in our unique moments and trying to have the same experience again, might not be appropriate. For example, consider the first trip to Disneyland with your family. Part of the tour, you probably experienced joy and excitement, you might even describe it as a magical moment. Travelling for second time to the same place, the experience will not be the same. It might better or worse, but different. This concept normally relates to the first-time experiences with a positive outcome, such as profession, falling in love, experiencing intoxication, completing a successful project, being 1st time buyer, winning a competition and so on. It feels like craving continuously for the initial pleasure, that may never occur in the same way as it happened for the first time.

Don't think just about happiness. According to research, the more we are trying to be happy, the less happy we become over time. Let me repeat the sentence. 'The more we are trying to be happy, the less happy we become over time.' But how is this even possible? 'Well, if I don't look forwards and want to be happy, how can I be happy?' Firstly, when you think just about happiness, it might create additional related pressure that may not be useful at the present. Secondly, it takes cognitive energy to think about it, so you manifest and address the happiness as a 'milestone' rather than an experience as you go along. Additionally, we fail to observe the life as it is, with its exposures as well as the difficult moments that are developed along the way. When considering happiness to be simply about beautiful or positive moments, we often neglect the unpleasant ones. This can cause more unhappiness, especially when we may feel puzzled or taken by surprise when some experiences may arise. Today is your last day of work before your holiday begins. In addition, you are celebrating 10 years of your marriage, which adds to your excitement for the day! Therefore, you are impatiently anticipating, so you can celebrate with your loved one. You might experience some challenges and unexpected circumstances at work, but not necessarily. In this case, the more you want the workday to finish, you will probably realise, the slower it goes. It often feels like the time stands still. However, by finding a different distraction, you tend to realise it becomes easier - probably subconsciously. It can be a tricky task not to think about it. One example amongst many others.

Expectations. Our emotional beliefs are shaped by our perceptions and interpretations of future situations or actions. As this happens, we begin to experience anticipatory feelings in advance. As soon as we book that vacation, we start to feel the way we anticipate that experience, the way it looks, whether we feel relaxed, enthusiastic or happy. Expectations can often be more satisfying than the actual experience. E.g. On a Friday - waiting for the weekend to arrive. For some people, this anticipation may start from Thursday evening or even earlier. Expectations shape our reality, what surround us, how to act and perform as well as the decision-making process. They are anticipations of how people perceive the world or consider what will happen from their point of view. They are based and formed from a genetic background, imagination, individual experiences, attitudes or personalities, and ultimately from the environment we live in. Expectations are realistic and unrealistic. Sometimes, these anticipations lead to a delightful and rich imagination. The mind takes us to places or scenarios that we never been before, such as world of dreams, surrounded by beautiful and glamorous places where everything is possible and comfortable. From time to time, it feels good, and it costs nothing. At the same time, they are considered a liability for a non-realistic approach. Suppose you've been thinking of running the marathon for some time and have decided to give it a try. For some reason, you believe in crossing the finish line with no time constraints. Excellent! As a note, you only went for a run two times in the last 3 years. Well, that's slightly delusional. A more realistic way may sound like. "A marathon has approximately 26 miles. It is a significant distance to run from a few attempts considering my limited running experience. I believe if I start with 1 mile at the beginning and gradually increase the distance as I go along, put the necessary effort in place while hoping that nothing or something unexpected happens during the journey, I might have a chance." When our expectations are higher than the reality we live in, they often bring disappointment and discomfort. "I was expecting my years of marriage to be nice, rosy and golden and they are not." Now, to several people this may look like: "You married the wrong person." "Well, it may be the case, but this is what I anticipated at the time!", "I thought if I have a job, a home, family around me, and be a good citizen, I will be happy and blissful forever, and I am not." Or "I know what my friend is thinking." Most likely you don't!

Expectations are normally formed from:

- Our imagination
- Environmental exposures
- Past vs future in relation to the present moment

Imagination vs reality. This occurs when expectations from our imagination exceed the expectations of reality. If you want to travel to x place, you cannot travel at the same time to y place or any other. An opportunity is omitted just because you made a simple decision. Even more importantly when x place didn't meet your expectations from the beginning. On these grounds, there is a choice to be made, and not all choices are weighed the same. Some hold a greater effect and consequence than others. Mostly, everything we do in our lives; we are exposed to more than one option. E.g. watching a film, how to spend our free time, dining out, choosing a job, and so on. How do we take the decision? On one hand, with the best intention, we select the one that we think is the most appropriate to us or is the right one. On the other hand, the same decision that we believe will make us happy, can also make us feel the opposite - unhappy. This is because we form expectations from our imagination, believing they will give us the best outcome and when they don't correspond to the reality, we are often confronted with disappointment. Technology doesn't help either in this case. It plays an important role by creating the objects to be more fascinating, captivating and interesting compared to how they actually are. From filtering to 'special effects' added to the photos, we often get caught into an idealised or distorted reality. The 'perfect world' of the social media is another contributing factor undermining an individual's happiness. Based only on a few fragments of reality, almost everyone looks happy, sharing glimpses of their best times or achievements, but not the day-to-day life's segments of tiredness, annoyance or fragility. For example, when we plan a holiday and hear about a specific destination from a friend or see it advertised online, we often find a place that appears attractive, beautiful. Therefore, we develop certain expectations of how inviting the place will be. Upon experiencing it, we may find that reality is much less attractive than the initial images we encountered. Usually, we tend to be happier when we explore the views for ourselves, where we don't maintain fixed notions and concepts, especially when we discover or experience something we didn't expect. A way closer to happiness, is whatever we are exposed to, whether is a service or an act of kindness, it's to come from the heart without self-benefit acts, nor having too many expectations in return. As the reality shifts from our expectations, the difference will often lead to disappointment even possibly resentment. To avoid this, a more convenient way is to maintain an evenly balanced ratio. Additionally, by improving our imagination, the reality we live in or reducing our expectations can be added to minimise the shifted gap. Of course, it's essential to have expectations that give direction and realisation, to accomplish any goals and aspirations, but we don't want to deceive ourselves or those around us.

Exposures from the environment. Environmental exposure has a great impact on someone's behaviour and happiness. Mainly because it's transmissible and we learn from one another, which becomes a new way of living. Our surroundings create a framework that influences how we act, discover, and perceive reality. In general, all the babies are born with a good sense of morality while expressing their temper through different ways of communication. As a note, genetic background doesn't play a significant role for example +/-5% difference as an inheritable contributing factor. This factor is largely uncontrollable amongst many others. Therefore, the toddlers in Croatia speak Croatian, the ones in Germany speak German and the list continues further to Brazil, England and so on. Later, what shapes us in life, is the family and society we are part of. When someone is exposed to a deceptive and dangerous society, there is a higher risk that they will adopt similar traits. The opposite applies when someone is exposed to a fair, compassionate and happier environment. This is because the environment we live in has a significant role in influencing behaviour and its effects can be transmissible and contagious. However, the person is still responsible for their own actions, as nobody forces them to act against their better judgment. The pressure to conform also serves as an additional contributing factor.

Moreover, when our expectations from the environment are not aligned with the reality we live in, we see and evaluate ourselves on what we encounter in the surroundings. If you have a higher wage than the average people and live in a poor neighbourhood, you will feel wealthy and well-off. If you earn the same amount but live in a rich neighbourhood, you will feel inferior and poor. If you get a 15% annual pay rise, it feels great.

If you get the same pay rise and everybody else in the team gets 25%, it doesn't feel so great. Nothing has changed. The initial state of 'feeling great' has changed instantly only due to a social context with others. This causes the individual to experience the opposite spectrum of feelings - dissatisfaction, disappointment and unfairness. The social comparison sometimes can be referred to as the Ebbinghaus illusion. The German psychologist Hermann Ebbinghaus discovered this illusion in 1890's. He described this phenomenon when a circle surrounded by a smaller number of circles appears to be larger, in contrast to another circle surrounded by a larger number of circles that appears to be smaller. In reality, the circles surrounded on each side are the same size. This illustrates how our perceptions can be influenced by the surrounding context.

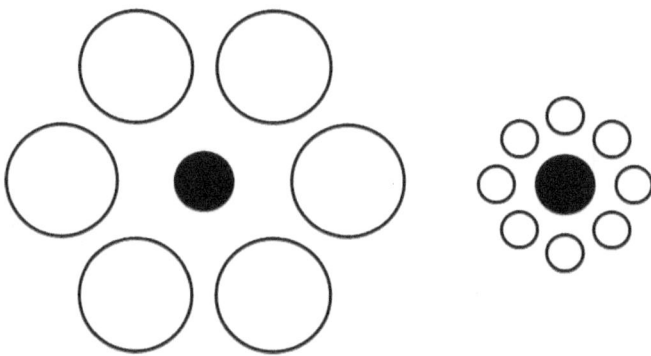

Ebbinghaus Illusion, the right-hand circle appears to be larger

With that in mind, our pain can benefit someone else, while someone else's pain may benefit us. The reverse is also applicable, our gain can become someone else's pain, and someone else's gain our pain. Sadly, one side loses and other wins. Someone's problem creates an opportunity for somebody else. Someone's health condition represents an opportunity for a medical practitioner.

Let's say, recently you haven't been feeling well, have experienced some abdominal pain, which led you to attend the local hospital. As soon as you walk into the main corridor to check in at the reception, you notice someone who has lost their vision, waiting for medical assistance. The first thought that comes into your mind, is to feel sympathy for that person and you wonder if there is anything you could do to help or support, you will be delighted to do so. The second thought that crosses your mind, however, is one of gratitude. You start to realise how fortunate and thankful you are not to be in their position, and this makes you suddenly aware that your problem is relatively minor. A different example involves a famous footballer who had no shoes to play football when he was very young. He originated from an impoverished family and often experienced pain, distress and numerous times he was in tears. At a later time, he encountered someone with a foot impairment, which made him realise how fortunate he truly was. On a different note, when love is present, it involves a different dynamic. Someone else's pain becomes your pain too. Normally, this is particularly evident in a parent-child situation, family or close relationships. If a family member has an accident or a critical disease, it becomes your suffering. The same applies for happiness. Someone's happiness becomes your happiness too: 'I'm happy if you are happy.'

Happiness is infectious within the group dynamic, whether it's your peers, a work environment or people you spend your life with. According to Harvard University studies, happiness is transmitted throughout the social community. More specifically, a next-door neighbour contributes as much as 34%, respectively 25% for a close friend. For example, having a happy friend increases someone's chances of experiencing happiness by 25%. This statistic comes with a 95% confidence interval, ranging from 1% to 57%. Additionally, if you saw someone ordering a dessert while you were dining out, there is a good chance that you will order one too. More interestingly, happiness is reached as a further expansion allowing an individual to spread their happiness through environment reaching up to 3 levels, friend of a friend. One day, my brother invited me over for dinner. We both live in the same city. He seemed quite enthusiastic about the invitation, although I wasn't sure why. He said: "Come brother come, I'll cook some dinner for us." I said, "Okay, I shall see you later." When I arrived at his place later that day, he was busy preparing the main dish. Driven by curiosity, "What are you cooking, if you don't mind me asking?" When we both grew up, my mother often made the same dish he was preparing, which we both enjoyed because it was a family tradition. But this time, it was different. He added two new ingredients to the original recipe. As we talked, I couldn't help but ask: "How did you come up with this recipe?" He explained: "Two days ago, I visited my uncle in another city. He and his wife invited me for dinner, while they prepared this dish, but with the additional ingredients. It was really good, and my thoughts were like, when I get home, I will do the same." I then asked, "How hungry were you?" "I was starving!" He replied with a touch of a smile. This is not limited to food only. Whenever something is seen while satisfaction is present, there is a high chance you will try it yourself at some point.

Present vs Future. Let's suppose: if you were to win at the lottery tomorrow, what would you choose? Getting the full prize in one lump sum or annual increments over the lifetime? According to the general population, most people tend to select the first option. When addressing the question: "Why did you choose this option?" Common responses include: "Well, a bird in hand is worth 2 in bushes"; "I could finally do everything I've dreamed of"; "It would grant me the financial and personal

Happiness, the premium desire

freedom"; or simply "I want to live and explore the moment, not in 15 years time"; "What if something bad happens few years later and I can't claim the full prize, I would feel extremely guilty and annoyed." These answers are regarded to be sensible and reasonable. Nonetheless, according to research, choosing first option for immediate gratification is driven by the short-term vision, which may lead to lower levels of happiness over time compared to those who choose the annual increments.

Which person do you consider to be happier? Person A or B?

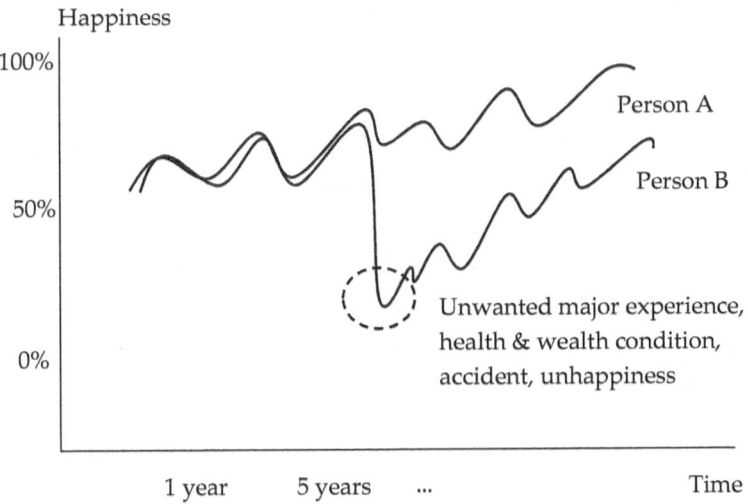

Life comes with a package, with ups and downs. During times of adversity, the past represents a portion of appreciation in the context of happiness when compared to the present moment. Going through a difficult period or recovering from a health condition represents a sign of resilience, especially when this is done in a timely manner. In this way, an individual becomes more tolerant to changes. The person then compares consciously or subconsciously the difference between the development of those changes. This often makes people appreciate the life more, and sustain a completely different perception about the world they live in. In addition, people cultivate a greater sense of purpose and a growth mindset, finding satisfaction and flavour over the *'smaller'* things in their lives. The new perspective would not be created if they would not go through the previous experience.

Gratitude is probably one of the best medicaments towards happiness in day-to-day life. It is purely an appreciation, a thankfulness for what we have, what is valuable to us rather than what we could potentially have. We may not have everything we wished for, but we have something. Perhaps we don't have enough financial funds, but we have a little. We may not have a large and cosy house, but we have a place to call 'home'. Perhaps we don't have an ideal life, but we have something that might be enough to live one. According to UCLA Research Centre, having an outlook with gratitude, has a significant conversion in our lives. By showing gratitude, does not only change the molecular configuration of the brain but also makes us feel better, happier while embracing what the wonderful world may offer at the time. You can nominate a few things that are the most valuable to you right now. How does it feel? With miniscule time and effort, by expressing gratitude, it improves the likelihood of taking care more of ourselves as well as taking the right path towards such entity. In other words, it increases the chance to show up more, to take more steps towards a healthier life, both physically and emotionally. Furthermore, it lowers the rate of unpleasant emotions such as frustration, envy, shame or feelings of inferiority. Expressing gratitude reduces social comparisons and judgemental errors of what we encounter in the surroundings while acknowledging others' achievements. Although it may seem effortless, practicing gratitude can be sometimes represent a challenging task, as people often focus on multitasking, lose themselves in daily activities, or consistently strive to achieve their goals and aspirations. Some people may consider it a 'weakness' associating it with lack of progress and development, as the person may not want to change something or be exposed to the risk of losing such belief. To cultivate such *requisite*, it's essential to feel the present, what surrounds us and feels tangible. Taking a moment to pause, perhaps smelling 'the flowers' can be a good alternative. From time to time, it takes experiences like traffic congestion to appreciate a quiet and empty road, sleepless nights to recognise a restful one, or dealing with unpleasant emotions to value the positive ones.

Laughing, which is a contributor of happiness, is highly transmittable. Approximately up to 30 times we are more likely to laugh with someone than by ourselves and then spread it to others. Media and advertisement companies make it easier in this case, by showcasing the most advertised and watched films, the images with most likes, or the hotel with the highest bookings. Often, if a large group of people likes a specific restaurant, there is a high probability you will too. Similarly, if an audience laughs at a comedy film, there is a good chance you will appreciate it too. However, there are different areas where this may not be applicable. For example, in the stock market. It works the opposite, when people recommend a specific company, you might not necessarily follow their lead. This is attributed to individual differences in perceptions and assumptions.

There are further various situations and circumstances that contribute to happiness. For instance, during a project, if the initial objectives are achieved or surpassed in terms of timeline, cost, or quality. If a project is completed ahead of schedule and under the budget by 20%, it can significantly enhance the overall satisfaction. Similarly, experiencing a good deal can boost happiness. Imagine visiting a local shopping centre while running into a pair of shoes that grabs your attention, but deciding not to purchase them for some reason today. One week later, you see the same pair of shoes with 50% discount price. It feels good, doesn't it? Dopamine may be released as a compensation.

Traveling offers a much-needed break from the daily routine and allows us to disconnect from our normal lives. Its aim is to help us "recharge the batteries" and engage in activities that differ from our everyday experiences. Traveling offers an opportunity to view, experience, and discover new ideas and perspectives that hold true value for us. Furthermore, traveling creates and abstract that we are not limited to just one place. Exchanging language skills, exploring new destinations, observing how locals live, and developing a broader perspective, are all part of the experience. During travelling, we are more likely to embrace new experiences, fostering moments of reflection and gratitude. This enables us to fully appreciate the present, especially when we compare it with phrases like "I knew it but didn't take the decision." It also opens our perspectives and allows us to develop a greater tolerance for the present reality. Washington University Researches indicate that travelling can contribute to a person's happiness up to 7%. Interestingly, when we travel on vacation twice per year it feels great, traveling every 2 weeks it doesn't feel as nice after a while.

Meaning. The assumption behind 'meaning' is repeatedly correlated as a twin sister to happiness. Various experimental studies suggest that behind the world 'meaning' is often blissfulness and happiness. It was initially promoted in 1946 by the well-known Austrian psychologist Victor Frankl. However, the term 'meaning' was highlighted under different circumstances throughout history and ancient civilisation. He is also the author of the book entitled 'The Man's Search for Meaning', which in 1959 become the best international seller. The book was primarily focused on how he endured the concentration camp during World War II by finding meaning in his life. He also developed logotherapy. In simple words, logotherapy is an effective method to enable individuals to discover their meaning in life. It's based on a therapeutic concept focusing on the ability to withstand a difficult situation through a search of purpose. Frankl believed that when we encounter a hardship that cannot be influenced or changed externally, then we should pay attention to ourselves. There were 3 interventions used in logotherapy: *Paradoxical intension* - a reasoning approach where the individuals were engaged to challenge and confront their biggest fears; *Dereflection* - a technique to balance worries and anxiety by changing deliberately the focus on different subjects; this approach was primarily developed in response to people becoming too blinded and obsessed with their thoughts or achieving their objectives. *Socratic dialogue* - a conversation approach to find out the effectiveness of someone's thoughts and behaviour. One of the main characteristics of meaning is through a life's purpose. To do that, Frankl realised that there were 3 fundamental ways towards such purpose: making a difference in the society, adopting courage through something difficult and by experiencing something to the greatest intensity.

Relatively, the happier we are, the more inclined we are to find meaning in our lives, and the closer we are to pursue meaning, the happier we are. This concept, however, is not always directly proportional. For example, individuals who have always had the desire to raise children, it would represent a sense closer to meaning, but on the same side a decline in their overall happiness. The meaning in this context is associated more on the self-concept, self-identity and cognitive processes, where the 3 dimensions simultaneously and constantly intercept, the past, present and future. Another characteristic of meaning is throughout passion where a person has a strong feeling and appetite to do something that becomes highly used almost daily. Leaving something 'behind' as well as having an impact on the society are not excluded in the meaning concept. Throughout history, many individuals have done so by creating valuable innovations such as the discovery of the light bulb, various mathematical formulas, and impressive structural masterpieces. These contributions are still visible after hundreds or thousands of years and continue to affect the society we live in today.

The idea of meaning sometimes emerges during times of change, which creates an opportunity for something else. A wonderful misfortune represents one of the best examples shown by Boris Cyrulnik's story when he experienced an extreme painful and life-distressing event. At the age of 5, he had a distinctive childhood having to go through life without parents. His entire family was killed during World War II. At an early age, Boris developed resilience like no other, which has motivated him to pursue his path in the field of neurology. In addition, his individual perspective and the memory of his parents have made him live only purposely and meaningfully from that moment onwards. This was to understand more what is behind the world resilience and to help people around the world when going through difficult events. Boris Cyrulnik focused on the key genetic aspects between a parent and a child, how those are interacted and manifested. He also emphasised on why a child is more vulnerable to a difficult event compared to another. More than 7 decades later, the French citizen is a pioneer in the resilience research centre. He spent his entire life in pursuing his meaning as a neurologist and psychiatrist to help people becoming more resilient throughout difficult life experiences.

Does **religion or spirituality** affect happiness? If yes, how? According to 'Handbook of Religion and Health', religion contributes to happiness in 78% of the cases out of 224 studies.

This is largely because people who tend to be religious are part of a group network and a community support centre. Religion also encourages people to minimise an unrestrained behaviour, while supporting wellbeing and cultural change. Mostly, religion inclines to offer people hope, a sense of meaning and purpose to deal with the daily obstacles and problems. Approximately 84% of the population are part of a religious community. This is diversified into Christians, Muslims, Hindus, Buddhists, and any other conventional religions. Religion is predominantly more intense in less developed countries because of the support and help provided by institutions, belief systems and hierarchy within the audience. Let's not forget, happiness can be contagious, so in this case religion too. If more people tend to follow a behaviour from others, this can lead to a bandwagon effect. In simple terms, individuals tend to adopt a conduct and conform to a situation purely because others are doing it. When it comes to spirituality, a person believes that there is something more than oneself or as a human being. It's often perceived as a deeper awareness beyond daily life experience. A person who embraces spirituality focuses less on the self-defences, the right or the wrong, with the aim of opening the heart towards every encountered scenario, welcoming and integrating different types of notions, emotions and experiences. Spirituality is frequently related to meaning, where a sense of purpose becomes common.

As happiness is expressed in many ways up to this point, another major part of it is to find it through our values. Values not only shape our life providing us a sense of direction, but also what matters to us, how involved and thoughtful we are with ourselves and others. When values are present, they often lead to satisfaction, fulfilment and happiness. Sometimes, they are identified as the individual's cognitive reasons that guide one's behaviour. Values are centred more on personal principles and qualities, while morals include those in correlation with the society we live in.

Values are significant influences behind a person's actions, reflecting our intentions in daily life. They are typically unique to each individual. One person may value privacy and respect while another kindness or integrity. Values are generated from beliefs, attitudes, and behaviours. How do we find our values? Sometimes, we don't have to do anything at all. The way how we interact within ourselves and with the outside world tells us nearly everything we need to know. If your colleague at work was treated unfavourably several times, and you felt irritated while witnessing this, one of your values could be fairness. This can lead even further to honesty and compassion. If you feel betrayed by your friend, you may value trust or loyalty, which was lost or undermined. There are also separate ways to identify our values that can relate to different aspects of life, including relationships, work environment and family. We can start by asking ourselves: What is important to me? What brings me satisfaction most of the time? What is something that I cannot live without? Other common examples of a person's values are punctuality, respect, autonomy, humility, family oriented, wealth, personal growth, dignity, friendliness, altruism, honesty, generosity and so on. Numerous studies have shown that being present and aligned with our values reduces stress and decreases the likelihood of being out of flow, stuck and confused, while contributing in a healthier manner to individual's self-esteem.

Authenticity is another form of value. Thomas, a financial consultant, works at one of the largest accountancy firms in the city. He's trying to do his job the best he can. However, when the company performs well or acquires new projects, he doesn't get enthusiastic like the other co-workers. He admits the reason for his contribution in the company is purely based on financial reasons. He is sometimes displeased, overwhelmed, and feels like he's in the wrong place. How long can Thomas stay in his job role? We all probably encounter examples like Thomas at some point, whether related to a job, a relationship, or other areas. If the way we think, feel and act is more present than not, it indicates we may attempt to an authentic and genuine life. Day by day, we are exposed to take hundreds of decisions, if not more. These decisions vary from a straightforward one such as: 'a black coffee with 2 sugars, no milk' to a more complex one: 'deciding your professional career', 'determining which employees should be laid off due to the new company's requirements' or 'relocating to a different country for a new job and opportunities'. In these choices lies the honest and authentic path we want to follow. Of course, being authentic, doesn't necessarily mean we adhere to self-serving scenarios where everything else is discounted and overlooked, but a compromise where we made that decision because we wanted to, rather than being imposed upon.

Another important ingredient towards happiness is through **meditations**. They transmit a form of relaxation and harmony that allow us to connect deeply with the best versions of ourselves in the present moment and not limited. Meditations represent unique practices that help us understand and manage our thoughts and emotions, allowing us to make the most of them. There are various forms of meditations including activities such as singing, gardening, cleaning, painting, walking, solving problems amongst many others. Marcus Aurelius, the Roman governor, has done so during several 'writings' between 161 and 180 A.D. He is known as one of the greatest leading emperors in history. The autobiographical writings called 'The Meditations' were based entirely on his daily routine as an emperor as well as on self-improvement practices to become both, a better civilian and a leader. These improvement practices were based continuously on justice, goodwill, doing the right thing to further develop his own character. More precisely on the virtues and flaws reflected towards such entity in his ordinary life. The remarkable series of books is considered one of the highest achievements in ancient philosophy. They not only represent an outstanding recognition throughout the past but also offer valuable insights into an emperor's daily life. Marcus Aurelius was recognised for his philosophical attributes and wisdom. *"Soon, you will have forgotten all the things around you, and soon all the things around you, will have forgotten you."* As he was dealing with many unhappy and disobedient people, the idea was: there was no point in being cruel to people because someone didn't do what they were supposed to do, all of these will be forgotten due to limited time, and the things will forget you for the same reason. Marcus believed that a wise person needs to live in accordance with nature, fulfilling their moral responsibilities and obligations. He thought the philosophical background brings no contextual differences in the social hierarchy. For example, if nature or God controls the world, if you are an emperor – be a good emperor, if you are a slave – be a good slave. He was not afraid of pain, not afraid of death or poverty, only afraid of doing what's wrong, not meeting his moral obligations or losing control of himself. A man who was bound to do regardless of any circumstantial factors.

As the leader of the greatest empire at the time, he could have anything he wanted, having access to all kind of pleasures and desires if he wished to do so. Exposed to temptations like no other, yet he chose not to engage in them. Instead, Marcus Aurelius focused on living an honourable and virtuous life. His character was nothing but a deviation from the norm, restraining his temper and actions throughout his 19 years as a supreme leader. Remarkable! During his supremacy, Marcus Aurelius held power over anyone alive in that time. He could have killed

Happiness, the premium desire

anyone if he got sufficiently angry. Under these circumstances, the meditations represented manuscripts, a collection of reflections as a reminder, to restrain himself from his actions and power. This showed how Marcus Aurelius viewed himself not only as an emperor, but also as a human being who did not benefit from the authority he had. This made him so uncommon and continues to resonate with the readers today, remembered and recognised for his abilities for nearly two millenniums and probably many more onwards. The greatest of the Romans, the noblest of them.

One way he emphasised his writings was through the concept of *'Voluntary discomfort'*. He intentionally engaged in difficult scenarios from time to time to achieve both strength and resilience. He understood that only through difficult moments he was exposed to, he could become more adaptable and resilient in the future. These examples were not only cognitive but physical too. For example, sleeping on the floor, skipping meals, or adhering to a sleepless night. A mental approach used in a valuable way mainly for uncertainty to prepare in advance how he should deal with difficult moments when they arose. This was done particularly when interacting constantly with a wide range of people, from unhappy and rebellious civilians to various commanders, all while facing threats from the opponents. During his supremacy as an emperor, finding the time to write was just unusual and impressive. An exclusive way to turn the page upside down, welcoming and integrating different unrestrained behaviours by directing the question to himself on what he could have done better, to improve his awareness and practising patience, when patience was needed the most.

Another effective method was throughout *self-discipline*, a substantial method to overcome the greatest challenges as the greatest commander. Marcus Aurelius believed that distractions, short terms pleasures and temptations are completely normal as a human being. Instead, paying attention on the task at hand, acting virtuously and righteously was key, especially in circumstances of unwillingness, hesitancy and during the presence of any unwanted thoughts. Showing up in a regular way, distinguishing what truly matters at the time, focusing entirely with commitment and seriousness, were all part of the self-disciplined approach. To stay away from all temptations and distractions, Marcus Aurelius used the concept of delayed gratification. A sustainable method at a glance to observe what matters in the long term instead of following the interim impulses. He understood that the real freedom comes from a self-control behavior over the worldly temptations and pleasures.

Furthermore, Marcus Aurelius believed deeply and truthfully in concept known as 'dichotomy of control'. Often referred as the following quote: *"You have the power over your mind not outside events, realise this and you will find strength."* Over the course of two decades, he commanded and harnessed his mind throughout his meditations, focusing on what he could control while ignoring everything else and accept it, which was described by the phrase 'Amor Fati' – translated from Latin as the 'Love of Faith'. This concept was used to embrace fate, with its own attractiveness, with the aim of accepting life as it unfolds with the inevitable changes and suffering. This was particularly relevant in circumstances when something was uncontrollable such as the limited life, the presence of natural disasters, or the daily routine of encountering various barbaric actions from the allies or opponents.

One of the longest studies on human happiness was performed by Harvard University in 1938. It involved 724 families at the time. After 85 years, the research still goes on, from generation to generation. Some of the original families, now in their 90's, are still taking part in the study, which is currently led by Dr Robert Waldinger. The aim of the research emphasised on how human happiness was experienced and distinguished at different stages of life by the same people involved. Participants were selected randomly from different social backgrounds including low-income families, those from violent surroundings, or medical students within the vicinity. The study showed that from the total number of families, the most significant factor contributing to their happiness was based on the quality of their relationships. The relationships that made them happier and healthier with time. That's because the individuals with marital satisfaction were better able to share their life experiences throughout the journey for a common reason such as closeness, connectiveness and caring. Avoidance of isolation was also part of it. Relationships not only in a romantic way, but also family connections, friendships, and other social bonds. One reason for this finding is that relationships are not easily quantifiable, unlike monetary factors or specific achievements. People often prioritise meaningful relationships over significant life incentives like wealth, fame or status. For example, we are more likely to stay in a job where a meaningful relationship is present, where we feel connected, or appreciated even when a lower grade in wage is considered. In many cases, this brings more value to someone in the long run compared to the incentives based on a short-term boost. However, this study was conducted based on 724 families. To a larger extent, one of the life's paradoxes, is that when 'monetary' features are in someone's possession, they are no longer important. When not, they become a main focus of attention. This is because an individual will be able to act freely based on their own choices, which fosters autonomy allowing them to do more with their present time or in the future.

Inner peace. Living in a challenging world, stress or worries seem to be more and more widespread amongst the society we live in. It can have a severe impact on the individual and everyone else related. If we don't have inner piece, we are in conflict. Conflict based on a personal aspiration, the person we share the life with or what is important to us. Also the way within ourselves, how the architecture of our own beliefs is manifested: perhaps singing or resting. Inner piece is a *safe place* in our heart and our mind where mostly everything is allowed. To be vulnerable and uncomfortable, creative and enthusiastic, exposed to risky decisions, failure or achievements. To reason that we have done the best we could at the time without any traditional paradigms such as: "I should not have done that" or "I know exactly what is going to happen during that event." Simplicity adds a portion to the individual's inner peace in a cognitive way without the extended use of decorations and glitters. To demand or seek less attention especially in a world filled with distractions and excessive embellishments. Simplicity, also in the way of living, regardless of one's status, hierarchy or financial standing. When exposed to different options, we have the choice to select a smaller 'luggage', which is manageable and handy rather than a larger one that may be heavy and unsuitable. In this context, the smaller luggage represents something meaningful and valuable when compared to the opposite, quantitative and large. Another feature of the smaller luggage is that we can store it anywhere and everywhere. It doesn't need a lot of attention and care too.

Moreover, to truly appreciate moments of happiness, we should recognise the importance of sad and unpleasant experiences. These emotional states work hand in hand to achieve and sustain the symmetry looked for. For example, to find serenity often requires avoiding viewing events in terms of a binary outcome - success or failure. Besides all, aren't both outcomes part of life? Without one, the other loses its meaning, often missing the genuine spark that comes from these experiences. There are stressors that are beneficial in everyday life such as: adhering to a busier schedule to achieve our well-intended goals, changing jobs from time to time, planning a wedding, or following a healthier diet. At the same time, there are stressors that are less beneficial. For example, worrying about the rainy season, getting caught in traffic congestion, experiencing a sudden car breakdown or facing last-minute flight cancelations. There are also stressors rooted purely in our imagination. Same as anticipated happiness, "Today is Friday, I will go on vacation in a few days' time." This is because we look forward to events, in this case - the weekend or the holiday. This is largely due to the activities we can do in the free time based on individual premises. At the same time, we can also experience discomfort before the actual event. "I'm not going to get a pay rise so I am not even asking!" or completely fooled by denial: "I have absolutely no doubt that I will get the job, even though I don't meet all the requirements needed!" Every change we encounter presents an opportunity to improve something and eventually ourselves with it. Inner peace is also found on the basis of how we deal with the reality rather than the one from our imagination. When the reality is shifted from our imagination, it can lead to feelings of discomfort and disappointment. Consequently, we have the tendency to do something about it. It sounds like a natural reaction to protect ourselves. When it gets too difficult, we will try to destroy any unwanted feelings or thoughts until they become manageable. Normally, whenever we are faced with various challenges, we tend to react immediately in an attempt to push the feelings or memories away. By avoiding them, these emotions or memories are stored away and when a similar event takes place, we respond in a way to avoid the uncomfortable feelings at the start of that experience. "My neighbour keeps parking the car in front of my drive, I better have a word with them, nicely and politely." Inner peace is additionally a form of relaxation that allows us to transcend our feelings. This often lies in our choices and decisions when we encounter different scenarios. I remember asking a colleague, "You seem quite happy and in a good mood today. Is there a particular reason for that?" The answer: "We started the day in a dramatic way, completely hectic with countless tasks to complete, and not enough time or resources. The situation seemed out of control. Currently, that's the only way to deal with such circumstances." Interesting…! The person shifted their behaviour in the opposite direction in response to the actual situation. Most likely, the brain is doing its job, sometimes - when feeling stressed, facing a challenge or even during a state of exhaustion – the mind employs different evaluation techniques adjusting our behaviour, actions and thoughts without even realising. It is the mind's way to protect and care for us. It could be a form of denial, which can be valuable to us in such situations. Thoughts like, "It's not as bad as I thought it was!"

Another way to achieve the premium desire is through **autonomy**. Autonomy - more in a sense of the inner self, rather than external part of us. To be able to feel and act the way we want, whenever, and wherever we choose. One reason behind autonomy, is because it aligns with the things that are important to us, satisfying and passionate. Things that are pleasant because of our natural attraction to them, rather than the external influences such as academic compliance or social conformity. An individual experiences autonomy when they act according to their own will, without concerned about emotional, financial or other forms of satisfaction. Furthermore, it involves adhering to one's own morals, beliefs, and goals. When this ability to act freely is threatened, physically or emotionally, an individual's happiness is then undermined. Autonomy aligns with the concept of freedom, as both involve a person's choice to control their own life. Emotionally, this has a huge impact on someone's happiness and life satisfaction. For example, when an individual has something to say – meaningful or not, free of self-expression or self- regulation. Or perhaps when they want to change something for the better. On the physical side, the individual's freedom is equally important, especially when someone's freedom is threatened or restrained. When it comes to detention, regardless of their guilt or innocence, it can severely affect their happiness. This impact is often intensified by stricter rules, limited rights and solitary confinement. This happens due to a number of reasons, a person may feel a temporary loss of identity, experience exposure to violence and confront unpleasant actions to a larger extent than normal. Being away from loved ones and ultimately the lack of virtuous acts in the environment can further diminish one's sense of autonomy. The presence of neutral colours with no natural light and a high sense of boredom are also factors that contribute to someone's sovereignty.

Another reason that I found attractive to list it in the happiness sector. For example, financially, if an original price of an item drops 50%, then shortly after it goes up 25%, I am happier than I was before despite having a negative balance of -25% over the course of a week. One of the countless examples available. Is it because I already made my mind up for the initial loss, or is it because of the most vivid experience, which is a positive one? This idea can also be extended to wellbeing, career development, or the society we live in.

Considering another example. Oliver, in his 40's, has seen his income gradually decline over the past years, while Samantha, also in her 40's, has experienced a steady increase in her income over the same timeframe. If the average is considered over the past years, their earnings are equal. Research indicates that Samantha is happier than Oliver despite those earnings. When the past is compared to the future and continuously progress as we go along, regularly improving or being better than the previous year, can lead people to be happier. The opposite is valid in Oliver's case, the experience of declining income affects his happiness and not positively. The difference in happiness appears linked to the perception of progress over time. In this case, happiness is measured not only on financial resources or income, but also on professional experience, relationships, wellbeing, productivity, amongst other themes.

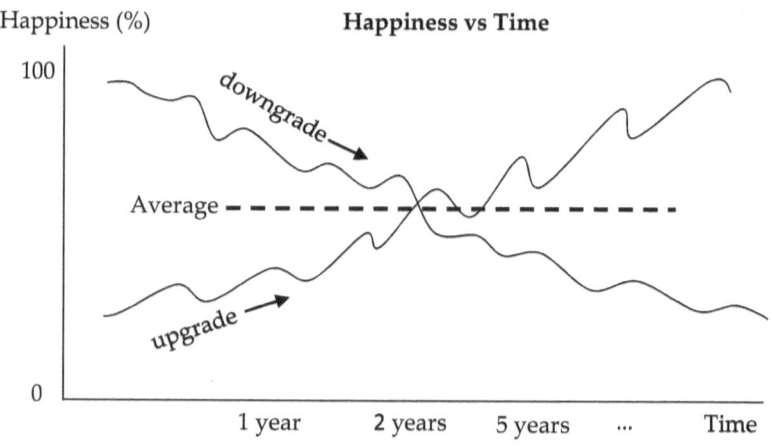

Sometimes, during a conversation, we witness various phrases or paradigms that people commonly use such as, "I want to be happy." This statement may seem self-explanatory, as we all probably share the same intention. This is what we want eventually, and along the way. However, the true meaning of "happiness" can vary greatly from person to person. When we encounter such requests, it's important to be more specific about the subject of 'happiness'. That's because happiness is extremely vast and has different meanings behind it. It's like saying, "I want to be good at sports." Is it football, gymnastics, darts? For this reason, it's important to be aware what lies under the word 'happiness' and how this is integrated in one's life. Being aware of the nuances behind the word "happiness", we can choose to be more attentive when picking the right words and to take actions towards achieving it, no matter how small those are. This can be done through some of the activities that make us happy that are proven through research and studies. Practices like expressing gratitude, using different breathing techniques or promoting the release of happy hormones, without becoming too obsessive with achieving an ideal state of happiness.

When reframing a statement into a question, consider the difference between asking "Are you happy?" and "Are you satisfied with your life at the present?" The first question often triggers ambiguous responses. Most of the times we say 'yes' even though that might not be the case, because the definition of happiness can be vague and tied to various experiences or expectations. This is likely to raise additional questions. In contrast, the question "Are you satisfied with your life at the present?" is easier to answer. It allows no room for a broader perspective when it comes to the specific moment. Satisfaction can be absorbed by good moments at the time, feeling productive, or simply lost by joy or relaxation. This applies not only to personal reflections, but also to inquiries regarding other subjects such as relationships, career, financial reasons and others. Clarifying questions can lead to more meaningful and honest responses.

The following approach is highlighted in later chapters, so I considered to apply it in this context of happiness. More specifically, using the inversion approach. For example, what does it take to make me unhappy? Staying inactive and indoors most of the time, eliminating the involvement in any challenges when they appear, staying in a comfort zone for a long period, loss of freedom, committing to something against my own will, full of resentment, high usage of alcohol and other harmful substances, holding unrealistic expectations, not having something to look forward to, the availability of no income, focusing on things that are uncontrollable from Mother Nature, not looking after myself, not learning something new, being stuck in the wrong job, taking life too seriously, expecting perfect fairness, unable to take a decision when facing numerous options, not being responsible for my own actions, continually thinking about past mistakes without a correlation for future references, exposed to violent and dangerous acts that treats both physical and emotional wellbeing and more. If those can be avoided, things will work in a half decent way…

Happiness can also be correlated with the imaginary puzzle that can never be entirely constructed, because of the missing piece or pieces.

II
Going through difficult times

They say when you go through a painful time or suffering, you should feel 'lucky'. Sounds superficial, right? How can we feel this way when something falls apart?! At the time, you probably don't realise, and unforgettable, behind pain and suffering there is often love, devotion and caring. Only then, when hurt and pain are present, we start questioning ourselves: Who is the person I want to become? What is the meaning of all this? What are my strengths or flaws? What do I really want for the rest of my life? Just a reminder to ourselves that our presence in the universe isn't forever. During this time, you may feel that the world runs against you, where everything feels unfair or confounding, but at the same time it makes us realise what is truly important and not.

When you go through an intensive experience negatively, you often feel exhausted, persistently sad, while interest and pleasure are no longer present. This normally happens during a tragic incident or a major change we don't want, whether it's the loss of loved one, having a significant health condition or witnessing one, going through a divorce, taking a big financial loss, losing a job or just doing something repetitive over time without sense and meaning. Unfortunately, we all confront some of these scenarios at some point in our lives.

Continuous pain or experiences of stress can have a severe effect on our lives, preventing us from living at our best. When this happens, the thinking and feeling process affect both emotional and physical state. The imbalance in the release of hormones such as serotonin and cortisol, makes it harder to perform, where we begin to lose appetite including an interruption in the sleeping pattern. A sense of taste or flavour begins to vanish. In a larger scale, it can further make us to go through the phases of pain or grief. According to Elisabeth Kubler Ross, a Swiss-American psychiatrist, there is a process how we manifest when experiencing something painful. This process has 5 fundamental stages. In 1969, she wrote the book 'On Dead and Dying', when she was observing patients who were diagnosed with terminal diseases. The stages are the following: *Denial, Anger, Bargaining, Depression, Acceptance*. Over the years, this process was adjusted to some extent where additional phases were developed and enhanced.

Denial. This is the first thing that comes into our mind and what we experience naturally. In other words, the shock we face during something tragic, painful or an unpleasant surprise. Simply, we refuse to believe what happens at the time, phrases like: "It cannot be true." "You are joking, aren't you?" "The diagnosis is wrong, they will call me tomorrow to inform me.", "This is a dream, soon I will wake up and nothing has happened". Alternatively, a person in denial mode may pretend that everything is okay, when it isn't. This phase serves as a defence method before we deal with the real pain. The mind tries to protect us in this case, only absorbing information, and feelings we can process and cope with. Additionally, this phase is intended to allow us more time to understand what really happens before moving to the next stage.

Guilt. When something bad happens, guilt is an emotional experience where we think we haven't done the best we could at the time, or because of us 'the change has occurred'. We begin to self-reproach by saying, "It's all my fault", "I should have spent more time with the loved one" or "I shouldn't have done that." This feeling can arise from both, the actions taken or not that could have changed the outcome of the event. Most of the times, the correlation between the individual and the event doesn't exist, being completely independent. Feeling guilty may be experienced along most stages, which can alternate between denial and depression. However, this phase is primarily distinctive to each individual and it's influenced by the specific change. While feeling guilty is a painful emotion, it serves a purpose too. It helps us to acknowledge our actions and intentions, reflect whether we did something wrong, improve ourselves or avoid repeating the same errors next time.

Anger. When compared with the 1st phase, anger is considered a hiding mechanism. We begin to understand the scale of the situation. The pain intensifies and rapidly increases under this phase. Now, almost everything feels irritating, what your mother-in-law told you 10 years ago, about your partner, your boss, the weather conditions, the food, the parking etc. Everybody else is found to be at fault, but not you, while you may lose control of your feelings - "Where is God when I need him the most?", "Why is this happening to me...?", "How did I even trust you!", are a few examples. During normal times, when the intention is to remain rational, this stage becomes too strong to act or think in that manner.

Bargaining. In this stage, the individual wishes to be back in charge of their thoughts and feelings. They may express thoughts like: "I wish I could go back in time to change this or do more!" Unfortunately, that's not possible. In addition, the use of 'if' expressions and scenarios is frequently common. Mainly, a negotiation has just started. "If x had happened, this would not have occurred." For some, especially those with religious beliefs, there may be a tendency to negotiate with God in exchange of relief from their current situation. A person often makes various promises to deal with their sorrow such as, pledging to become a different person or to help others more. The bargaining phase also serves to give the individual more time, as feelings of uncertainty and vulnerability are becoming more intense.

Depression. This is when the real pain starts. You begin to feel exhausted, overwhelmed, continuously sad, with no pleasure found in the activities you were once after every day. Withdrawing from others, feeling lonely, adhering to self-neglect signs, and finding it difficult to make decisions, are separate feelings within the individual's experiences. Sleeping more or less than normal represents another feature. These feelings have a profound impact on the individual, where physiological, emotional and sometimes cognitive functions are affected, where a person may feel stranded and helpless. Often exposed to phrases like, "Why even bother?", "I wish tomorrow can all go away', "What do I do now without him/her?", "Life is so miserable." This is the most painful stage in the grieving process. The aim of this stage is to develop different scenarios to manage the pain. If you feel you can't get out of the situation or don't see an improvement within a few weeks, additional help might be required in this case, such as cognitive behavioural therapy or someone you can trust without being inclined to prejudice or critics.

Acceptance. After the 'black hole' experience, feeling trapped and hooked, the sun starts to come out. The person's aim is to accept life as it is, accepting the pain, while trying to find a way to move on. Common thoughts and sentences, "There are more days in the front of me," "I tried my best, there was nothing else I could have done more", "I am not the only person going through this case", "It's all part of life, it happened for a reason" are often used. Once the individual is willing to accept the situation, they look forward to different approaches that can be used to live with the pain and look for alternatives or possible solutions to continue with their lives. The acceptance stage does not necessarily mean that you are completely withdrawn from the changes or painful time but instead consider it as part of life and who you are, what it actually means, while recalling the good moments not just the unpleasant ones. Often, this phase encourages a balance of reflecting on both, what went wrong and right.

Integration. After reaching the acceptance stage, a person gets a little more relaxed and begins to settle into their new reality. Now, the main aim of the individual is to integrate back in society. The motivation slowly gets back on track. This may include trying new interests, finding things to look forward to, adhering to a schedule, connecting with others, applying for a job or changing one, what does it take to complete plan A, and more. The person starts to experience a sense of the new reality. It doesn't happen overnight, it might take some time, where patience and prudence could be the key ingredients.

These stages are intended to help us to navigate through pain or stressful moments while we adjust and conform to the 'new' normal life. However, everyone may experience the change differently, in a more personalised way, and not following a particular order. The time spent in each stage depends on the situation at hand respectively on the individual, which can vary from weeks to months or years. Additionally, the experience itself is unique, as the individual's traits, environment, and people around can have a significant influence. Some people may get stuck in the depression stage for a longer period. However, to 'qualify' for a state of depression, an individual must confront the feelings or symptoms for approximately 2 weeks continuously or more. This is not when someone is disappointed when they didn't get their promotion wanted, experiencing frustration from

Going through difficult times

a last-minute flight cancellation, feeling sad from time to time, or having a late night with your friends and feeling 'hangover' next day.

Grieving is an entire process when experiencing something painful, while depression is a stage, the most painful one within the grieving process. Depression is identified separately as a medical condition. In this case, some of the stages might be skipped. The grieving process is associated to a significant loss. It occurs during the presence of love to someone or something and no longer after. Depression's trigger points are more related to oneself and self-identify reasons but not limited. For example, small irritation points built over time, genetic background, or by the chemical imbalance of the neuro-biological hormones. Cortisol hormone for stress handling and serotonin as a mood stabiliser. However, both conditions share common symptoms such as sadness, tiredness, lack of motivation, overwhelming thoughts amongst others.

According to World Health Organization, depression is considered one of the leading disorders amongst cancer, hepatitis, heart stroke, diabetes, and any other diseases. A subject that has received much attention for the last decade. It's commonly identified as a limited capacity for a more severe or clinical depression where some of the basic functions are impaired. For instance, doing your daily activities can be a real challenge. Approximately 5% of the entire adult population are affected by it. Quite a substantial number. I believe it's an important topic, despite being contemplated not an open subject most of the times, where people are often restrained to express themselves in this realm. Factors such as genes, bodily hormones and the environment influence the pain scale. There are further causes and cases that can contribute to grieving or depression. This could be associated to post-birth conditions, during physical or verbal abuse, thinking styles, extensive usage of alcohol and drugs, childhood experiences, experiencing a natural disaster or war, miscarriage, constantly thinking about past mistakes, loss of freedom, toxic relationships, working on a problem for a long time and not finding a feasible solution, small irritation points built over time, constantly sensing that you put too much in something and are not rewarded appropriately, feeling like going backwards not forwards with a personal timeframe, high level of loneliness, failure after failure after failure with no favourable outcomes in between and many others. When it comes to the last example, this cycle can be interrupted from time to time and turned into a real success. Marlon James's novel written in 2005 was rejected seventy-eight times before it was published. The book named *John Crow's Devil* became an inspiration after so many rejections. He consequently accomplished the Booker Prize of the year.

Everyone can experience grief and painful times at some point in their life. Can it be prevented somehow? It's certainly not a preference, where we decide whether we want it or not. In opposition, if the person has done something intentionally, it might be a potential consequence where the feeling of guilt can become the main reason. It's predominantly considered as being 'out of control', especially when someone goes through a significant change in life. If you discover that one of your siblings or parents has a terminal disease or suffered an accident, I believe it's normal to have those symptoms. This is how we show up when love is behind, something important to us was lost or might be threatened. Numerous times, there is a misinterpretation between the actual word described and recognising what we genuinely feel, failing to observe the real meaning of it. Primarily, the statement of words that can be incorrectly associated with higher emotional impact than normal. 'Big words' such as strained, overwhelmed, fed-up, exhausted, depressed, stressed, disgusted or angry are commonly expressed. Instead, we may feel tired, lonely, bored, irritated, confused or hesitant. When you had a difficult conversation with your partner and you felt frustrated, perhaps a disagreement mode is more realistic, or the message was poor from your side or not understood by the other. Additionally, when trying to solve a problem while not finding an interim solution and feeling 'overwhelmed'. Instead you could feel 'uninspired' based on different influencing factors at the time, such as loudness or tiredness. The reverse applies too, when you go through something tragic and painful, you might downplay your feelings by saying, "It's fine, not a big deal, it's nothing...", assuming that you are not in the denial mode pretending that everything is okay.

Labelling our emotions correctly can be fundamentally important, helping us to detect the actual cause. It not only plays a valuable part in being closer to what we genuinely experience, but also provide us with a more likely solution to deal with the problem at the time. Often done unintentionally, mislabelling regularly brings confusion, an unknown gap between ourselves and the possible effect when facing a challenge. Naming our emotions and feelings in an appropriate manner can reduce the impact of stress or difficult emotions while giving us a clearer and more transparent way of understanding what happens at the time.

Time and time again, people are exposed to sentences like: "Get a grip on yourself and move on," or "How long are you going to continue like this?" While these statements are often made with good intentions, they can come from anyone, someone we don't know, an acquaintance, a colleague, or a close family member. Sometimes, we witness a more traditional one: "Just be positive, everything will be fine!" If this will solve all the problems at the time, there will be no health disorders in this world nor any other related topics, no need for physicians, doctors or medical centres since it's a self-curing process. It might help in some scenarios as 'something to look forward to', but instead we want to be more realistic, not to deceive ourselves, to be more exposed to disappointment and discomfort. In many circumstances, staying positive on false premises can make the situation worse. Even looking positive at the time, this can be attributed to self-emotional detachment. When a person is going through painful times and exposed to such phrases, it creates a difference between the actual feelings and what they are expected to feel as if it was nothing, failing to be understood. An individual may feel even more pressurised to behave in another way.

In opposition, when we experience painful emotions and the need to respond whenever an answer is necessary: "Everything is fine and well!" - doesn't help either. On one hand, we pretend that we are okay but on the other, not showing the actual feelings. This is different from when we fail to accurately label our emotions, which is done unintentionally or not choosing the right vocabulary, while in the case of emotional separation we acknowledge our feelings but not express them in an authentic way. Probably, we don't want to show signs of weaknesses, either to ourselves or to the outside world. Expressing emotions in a transparent and genuine way can help the individuals to be more honest with themselves, allowing them to navigate their experiences as they truly are. Under some conditions and with a sense of balance in mind, just because last evening's dinner didn't taste as you wanted, and the new shoes you ordered arrived in a different size, the entire world needs to know.

On many occasions, during painful times, one problem can lead to another. There is probably a mark left behind during those experiences, and now once integrated back in society you may start the new chapter from a different 'reference point'. For example, going through a divorce, or dealing with a serious health disorder, the relationship may be at risk, the financial situation, the job, and more. It can be extremely challenging to perform at your best ability in the current job while observing a family member has a critical health condition or a terminal illness. Similarly, going through a divorce while arranging children's custody is another example. At the same time, these circumstances can serve as a 'preparation' for the real-world scenarios, as life itself can be the best educator, professor and facilitator. A good example is during pregnancy. During the last phase, a female develops symptoms such as troubles sleeping, mood changes, continuous worries becoming a mum and how to cope with the newborn. If not, it could be feelings of providing, caring or just excitement to such scenario. These symptoms are considered 'signs' before the child gets born, as the body and mind become prepared for the new event.

Sometimes, intense depression causes more stress, and in turn, more stress and worries affect the depression even more. This is known as rumination, when the person alternates from one to another in a vicious cycle. Rumination is considered an overthinking and overwhelming process, where a person goes over and over the same thoughts most of the time. These thoughts are identified as distressing ones, generated from past, present and future. They can involve constant worrying, doubtfulness, vulnerability, uncertainty, and continuous sadness. Sometimes, it feels like paddling up the river stream and no progress is being made, no matter how much effort is assigned. Depression is linked to past experiences, while stress, in general, is an emotional reaction initiated by different causes. These triggers are generated from current and future situations. Stress also comes from ignoring the actions which a person has control of by setting them aside, instead of the actions that are difficult to manage. Worries are normally originated from future scenarios without the need of a particular cause. One way to reduce the effects of rumination, is to observe your thoughts and understand what you are experiencing. A different way is to shift the attention somewhere else. Similarly, in the case of Victor Frankl to find meaning in the concentration camp, where he used dereflection as a distraction tool, when his thoughts were becoming too strong and too intense.

In the event of experiencing an unwanted major change or facing a difficult situation, a good starting point is to allow your feelings to flow naturally and navigate through the process. Below are some activities that can help to some extent dealing with difficult times, particularly those that are within a person's control:

- Understanding what you are going through
- Feeling exposed to gratitude. This is not easily applicable as the person may not be in the right emotional state. Trying to be grateful for you, people or things which are still valuable to you
- Don't fight your emotions or feelings
- Asking for help
- Engage in breathing techniques. It's currently proven through research that breathing can help towards the adjustment of biological hormones
- Writing down the experiences you encounter
- Taking 'baby steps' and one day at a time
- Identify some of the trigger points and adhere to small manageable actions or decisions

- Trying to remember something positive, productive or feeling good moments. It hasn't always been like that, nor will be - painful and gloomy
- You shouldn't believe everything you think is true. The mind might take you to various places or situations like no other, having overwhelming thoughts which can alter how the reality is perceived. These are not facts nor true information.
- Adhere to small treats and self-compassion approaches
- Integrate any of the activities that you once found pleasant back in the daily routine
- Meditation and spirituality are identified as different ways for a calmer mindset to support the individual

Meeting the right people at the right time has a valuable contribution in the way a person sees and absorbs life, especially in pain, loss or suffering. Many people may not have the opportunity. This could be anyone, someone unknown or close to you, a work colleague, or the local GP. There could be simple gestures such as an act of kindness, an understanding of what a person experiences, a memory shared, listening with the aim of understanding, being supportive, sharing something amusing, or purely just the way they are, how they present themselves to the world, without doing anything specifically.

Unhelpful Thinking Styles

Every day starting from an early age onwards, we all sustain some of the abstract thinking models, the way we interact with ourselves, others, or in any given situation. Thus, different ways of thinking are sustained or changed as we go along. When dealing with various scenarios or challenging times, our mind attempts to understand and translate, what we go through and what happens at the time, providing us with one or more potential solutions. One method is to adhere to 'shortcuts', a simplification in our mind to reach quickly to conclusions, choices and decisions. The following thinking styles that are often used can alter our perception of the reality. Most of them are used to feed the pain scale, especially when someone goes through a difficult period in life. They are identified as unhealthy, more applied in a negative way, but not necessarily. These unhelpful thinking styles can also form a habit in the daily routine, due to their high usage over the years.

Mental filtering. This thinking style happens when we only pay attention to the information we want to see, by filtering one side of the information and discount everything else. This typically is applied more in a negative way. For example, "You have dinner with your partner, and the waiter drops something by accident on your shirt". The entire night you start focusing on the unpleasant moment with the shirt, instead of enjoying the pleasant experience all-round. Another common example can be found in receiving feedback from your current job or in any related context. The feedback is overall positive, where one or two points need a little bit more attention. Instead of absorbing the information as a good result, your focus is only on one point that makes the complete feedback to be inadequate or poor. Nonetheless, when a person receives a response that most of the points require attention, the person still engages on the overall result leading to an ineffective response.

Mind reading. This concept refers when we imagine what someone else thinks, mainly about us, without any specific causes or reasons. Examples: "If you are late 5 min for your work schedule, you consider that everyone is thinking that you're late." "If I do x, others will think such and such", "Wearing a different outfit for a party theme - you think what others are thinking about your outfit, making you feel uncomfortable." "If I don't deliver the presentation in a high standard, it will make me look foolish in front of the audience." "Going out on a first date, and someone is slightly quiet, you start thinking, he/she doesn't like me, they get bored!" In other words, an individual makes an assumption without evidence and the practice of communication.

Jumping to conclusion. As the name indicates, an individual jumps to a conclusion too quickly without enough information to verify the concept. Also, it relates to the 'mind reading' where the 'assumption' is the predominant factor. When you call your friend and doesn't answer within a short time, you start assuming they ignore you, don't care, are doing it deliberately or something bad has happened. Alternatively, the individual is exposed to a more predictive thinking, even overestimating their own abilities, thinking with preciseness of what is going to happen in the future, without considering any other information available.

Personalisation. Thomas and Jane began a long-distance relationship for approximately 1 year. Both are residents in separate countries. During the last discussion, Thomas decides to take the relationship to the next level. Indeed, with Jane's desire and approval, they both come up with the idea and agreement that the best solution would be for Jane to move over. Thomas is a self-employed individual working for one of the largest firms in the city, specialising in civil engineering. Jane is a project manager in the energy sector. After living together for some time, Jane experiences some difficulties in adjusting to the place, working environment as well as to the new culture. After a while, things start to slip between each other, although being together and in the presence of love. Jane has some challenges at her current job, not being able to perform as she wanted. While witnessing this, Thomas feels completely responsible, and he often blames himself for everything that Jane experiences. He thinks, because of him, Jane is going through difficult times. Thomas feels overwhelmed, guilty and disconnected from the reality. On the other hand, Jane feels slightly irritated and finds Thomas responsible for her difficulties and experiences. The situation gets from bad to worse, where the detachment between each other intensifies. Personalisation occurs when individuals consider and blame themselves frequently, feeling responsible for everything that happens, even when they have no influence over a situation or without sort of involvement. In contrast, this form of thinking is also considered when some people feel completely irresponsible, despite their partial or full involvement, starting to shift the attention or responsibility to others for various reasons.

Catastrophising. A tendency when someone expects and assumes the worst possible case scenario in a given situation. In other words, exaggerating and overestimating an outcome with or without real evidence to support the initial belief. When a small error occurs, the person starts to engage in so-called 'a scanning for devastation'. For example: During an anniversary party, you had a line of reasoning with your partner. Now, you're beginning to think they might be fed-up and unhappy, no longer loving you, and possibly wanting to divorce. In a different example, when someone takes an assessment, the acceleration of thoughts rapidly increases, assuming in case of failure, won't follow any higher education, becoming unemployable and ultimately poor. Similarly, when an individual needs to present something in the workplace, and realised they caused a blunder. "If I don't deliver as I should, they will be dissatisfied with my work and probably I will be losing my job, and I can't find another job!"

Magnification and Minimisation. This refers to the tendency of people to magnify their errors or minor incidents as being more 'significant' in reality, while downplaying the good outcomes or accomplishments they achieve. A person drops a glass of water, which leads to a 'massive' impact and trouble, while receiving an A grade instead of an A*, feeling a 'failure' or incredibly annoyed. On a different note, this style is applicable, when individuals believe and assess others' achievements as being more valuable than actual, but when it comes to evaluating themselves, despite their own achievements, substantially poor or underachieved.

Repetitive Contrast. An inclination for individuals to compare themselves unfavourably with others on a persistent basis resulting in self-criticism as well as threatening their self-worth. "My friends are getting rich investing in company A while I get stuck in this 9 to 5 job." Thinking and comparing that other people are more intelligent, smarter, richer or prettier. This leads to frustration and discomfort when there is no need.

All or nothing. Also known as the 'black-and-white' thinking, this cognitive approach is a type of thinking when people perceive the world in the extremes, right or wrong, wonderful or disastrous, with no spectrum in between. Common words such as 'Never', 'Always', are frequently used when a person states their opinion about something. Based on a simple characteristic, a person engages in categorising something or someone, including themselves as 'exceptionally good' or 'complete failure'. If someone didn't say "Hi", the person might think they are a total disgrace, while receiving a compliment they think they are, 'incredibly polite and friendly' or, "If I don't get the job, I am not good enough, but if I do, I am exceptionally good".

Emotional reasoning. This thinking style implies that when we feel concerned or worried, the situation must be bad or dangerous. When the reasoning approach is used, it's identified as a mistake because it prioritises feelings instead of the evidence. For instance: An individual wakes up, had a weird dream, and feels worried. They look out the window, it's rainy and windy. Now, they begin to believe that today is going to be a bad day, or "I feel tired, so I need to find another job". Engaging in emotional reasoning may trigger the fortune telling approach. In this case, the individual may be exposed to unreasonable assumptions. Another approach based on predictive thinking. When someone assumes they will fail an assessment, this belief can prevent them from taking the necessary actions to prepare, which ultimately results in failure. After a few attempts, they believe the problem lies with them, even though is hot topic, competitive and challenging for most people. The self-fulfilling prophecy is another cognitive style associated to reasoning. This thinking methodology is manifested when someone imagines something will occur, simply because they believe it will happen. This can be applicable both, negatively and positively. For instance, when a person expects that the chances of being successful in a particular subject are limited or low, they will prepare less for that action.

Overgeneralisation. Sophie recently ended a romantic relationship after discovering that her partner had been unfaithful. Felling disappointed and heartbroken, she took some time to heal. She found herself in this situation only once. Eventually, she meets someone new and finds him attractive. However, while engaging in a casual conversation, Sophie suddenly recalls the painful memories from her past relationship due to a small unrelated topic. Although she has no evidence or real cause to suspect the new partner of being unfaithful, she gets easily irritated by saying: "They are all the same, they never change!" Regardless of her new partner's loyalty, overgeneralisation is found on the basis when someone makes a generic assumption for all possible scenarios when one is exposed only in a single experience or from time to time. Sophie's feelings are not unique, many people fall into this pattern. Common phrases that illustrate this pattern include "I always have bad luck" or "Nobody takes responsibility here", "All rich people are arrogant or too proud of themselves", "All politicians are corrupt".

Always being right. The tendency for individuals to seek and prove that an outcome is right, in their favour. While it can impact their self-confidence, when considering the bigger picture, most of the times it's irrelevant, depending on the subject matter. Opinions and facts are spread differently when making a statement about something. People perceive realities in different ways, instead of proving constantly that their story is the right one. However, this cognitive style is highly dependable on the discipline in which it's applied. For example, in a medical institution or engineering, it works on the principle of science, where accuracy and safety play their roles. In the law department, this is to distinguish the difference between what's right and wrong, while in social situations this concept is less dependent.

Judgemental errors. This is an unhelpful thinking style when people tend to evaluate themselves or others through critical and judgemental displays, without the ability to recognise what they genuinely observe. Dividing, extrapolating, and rejecting anything that threatens their point of view or perception. Individuals are often involved in circumstances by labelling and making inaccurate affirmations, about almost everyone they interact with. These errors are observed repetitive and at a high frequency level.

Ross Hodgkinson, a sales manager, found himself in this scenario, when he was too quick to fall under this cognitive error. While travelling to meet a client in a rough and impoverished area, he assumed he needed to hide all his belongings and expensive items from the car, because of what he considered at the time of the surroundings. He made this decision based on stereotypes he attributed to those in the vicinity. Based on this information, he believed he had a good reason to do so. However, upon meeting the client, Ross was pleasantly surprised to find them to be one of the most welcoming individuals he had ever encountered. The client left him a souvenir too, as an appreciation for his service. Therefore, Ross could not believe at that time, and he still remembers this story despite was 15 years ago. Although the experience is considered just a one-off scenario, that event taught Ross a valuable lesson to remember for long, refraining from assumptions too quickly before giving the opportunity to someone. As a result, he understood not to repeat the same behaviour in the future and to be more rational with himself and those around.

Research from University of Glasgow indicates that we form an opinion about someone in a fraction of a second, mainly if they are trustworthy and worth having the conversation further. This initial judgement is entirely based on physical characteristics, body language and how they represent themselves. Truly, this is not enough, to have any relevant conversation that may alter the way we see someone's demeanour. Other research debates the same subject up to 7 seconds. A little bit more realistic I suppose, but still not appropriate. This is based on the first image captured and oriented in our mind to make an evaluation of someone's likeability, trustworthiness and perhaps intelligence. This quick reaction is reflected as a self-protective mechanism. Sometimes, we might get it right, but many times also wrong. With that in mind, jumping to a conclusion based on a handful of seconds or less, without considering other relevant factors, failing to observe anything that might change the first impression, it does not promote a healthy way to ourselves.

Pollyanna principle. In its simplest form, this principle is described when people have the tendency to view the world in a more positive way rather than a realistic way. The term 'Pollyanna' originates back from the 20th century, which was a novel story written by Eleanor Porter. Pollyanna was an orphan girl who was constantly trying to seek positives by playing 'a glad game' in everything she was exposed to in her daily life. Many of us are inclined naturally to an outlook towards the positive. This is identified as a good way to cope with challenges and problems observed in certain scenarios. Nonetheless, when Pollyanna effect refers as an excessive optimism, it's a form of distortion or an unhelpful thinking habit. In other words, people tend to look at things far more positive than they truly are, what they are represented for and neglect everything else. Many times on the false premises and any other external circumstances that can influence the end outcomes.

Sometimes, during difficult times while adhering to some of these thinking habits, a person can express high accuracy in their own judgments. This thinking accuracy influences perceptions for a more realistic understanding in certain events. For example, when considering the subject of the national lottery, a person recognises this concept as an extreme low probability of winning, which is verified and proved through the theory of probability calculations. However, being too accurate in our judgments is not a sustainable way to living a healthier lifestyle.

We all experience some of these thinking approaches from time to time, some deeper on the spectrum scale than others. However, when they are used regularly, the situation changes. Instead, we don't want these ways of thinking to become habits, that drain our energy or serve as a deflection in our daily routine. There are times when these thinking patterns are effective, but retrospectively, when they become used consistently in an automatic way, they can cloud our perceptions, and distort the reality we live in. For example: the 'black and white thinking' aims to achieve a project goal more clearly and efficiently. Leaving no room for grey area, this approach can help reduce unnecessary debates, various obstacles and any superficial aspects of a project. A negative visualisation is a thinking approach that involves how unexpected moments will originate throughout the day or time, while preparing the necessary actions to deal with such scenarios. It's often considered a valuable method used for difficult moments and uncertainty to prepare in advance, allowing individuals to minimise the risk associated with those. When attempting to a 'mind reading' approach, we might think, "Something is distressing my loved one, despite saying "everything's okay." This perspective can lead to a reasonable conversation, on why they are upset, allowing them to feel heard, supported or showing compassion when needed the most. When it comes to catastrophising, where the acceleration of thoughts spirals rapidly in anticipation of failure, can signal the need to take different actions to avoid such scenario. Alternatively, it influences someone's happiness as the situation can only get better when compared to the initial belief. Self-fulfilling approach may kick off in some cases to help the individual to increase the likelihood of success involved in a specific subject. In scenarios where we insist on 'always being right', recognising our mistakes provides an opportunity to learn something new.

One way to challenging these thoughts or patterns is to identify them and question ourselves: How did I come up with this solution? Is there any evidence related to support my thinking, ideas or behaviour? Could it be an alternative way of thinking?

Why do I focus on only one piece of information? Is there a more sensible way of reasoning these scenarios? When addressing those questions, we become more aware of the circumstances, giving us more time to respond, a more plausible way of thinking and respectively a more realistic solution.

I try my best, sometimes I fail...

I thought to start with the following sentence: *"Everything in moderation, including moderation!" - a* philosophical quote promoted by Oscar Wilde in the 19th century. Wilde's perception behind this phrase was to keep a balance of all things including the balance itself. It was based on a thinking approach and outlook of how something is handled before and after an event. The quote promotes the concept of balance between everything we do in our daily life. Between a self-restraint conduct and high attraction when it comes to a trait of indulgence. Between brutal honesty and total falsehood. Between high commitment and low imprudence. Between an unused potential and a fertile skill. Between obsession and reluctance. In other words, to be more open to a line of moderation that lies between them. At the beginning, 'Everything in moderation' surely does not represent the right concept when dealing with many daily activities or plans. It cannot be practical in a broad context. We certainly want less moderation in some areas, for example - resentment, criminal acts, dishonesty, and more of the other side - becoming more helpful, having more walks in nature, exercising or reading more. The second context makes it a lot more practical, 'including moderation', which is not excluded in the sentence.

When a line of balance is present for longer, we naturally tend to go back in the search of stimulus. This makes us to involve in any activities or challenges, becoming either too preoccupied or devoted to accomplishing any set goals. Whenever we encounter these scenarios, we want to return to the original state, a state of tranquillity and harmony, which is normally done through comfort and relaxation. The uncertainty and the unexpected play their part, as life itself is unpredictable to changes. Changes in the environment, time or within ourselves. If something is used too much it can become harmful, if used too less - it might not be enough. It's a non-linear concept, the right amount depends on the individual premises in context with time. When remaining for too long in those modes, it has its own concerns, we become less resilient, unable to tackle any issues or challenges, or to reach any personal goals. To find that line of balance in everything we are exposed to as we go along is extremely difficult to achieve.

Various opportunities could be uncovered depending on what we do, see and observe. At the time, we don't know if something represents an opportunity. Often, these opportunities come hand in hand with threats that can derive from different aspect of life including wellbeing, personal matters, financial concerns and professional challenges. Whenever we identify an opportunity, how can we determine the best course of action in a given situation? We don't, we think we know and hope to take the best possible approaches and decisions, but we are still not certain. The end outcome still allows room for debate. During these opportunities or changes, most people want to see radical variations. Variations with great result for better or worse. In the case of opportunities, most people demand in no time to see significant positive effects that result from them. The opposite applies too. In times of adversity, individuals desire to return to their original state immediately as if nothing ever happened. Truly, that's not a bad thing to crave for. Yet, because of these radical variations the process is often delayed, prolonging the sorrow or hindering success. In this context, being more rational with ourselves plays a significant role to deal with such opportunities, changes or challenges. It's identified as a reasonable approach in our mind and our actions based on what is presented to us at that moment in relation to the environment we live in. Alternatively, when something becomes overwhelming or obsessive, distraction can be a valuable strategy. Sometimes, adopting a self-reflection attitude allows us to recognise what went wrong and right, not only in the past but for future improvements too. We can therefore integrate those experiences in our life as we move forwards in a more natural and effective way. Whenever we are involved in a project, halfway through we realise that the risks and consequences associated with it are increasing exponentially. These high implications could affect personal wellbeing, financial metrics, relationships and other areas. What do we do? Should we push the boundaries further at a given price or take a step back and accept the pain? Again, along the way, we still don't know how the outcome will unfold every single time. In a world where competition rises in almost any discipline, if we are faced with a zero-sum game, how do we show up to that event? Do we strike for the winning hit, or do we perform by avoiding mistakes? Like a tennis player… We might also consider making small improvements over time if there is time. I wish I had a magical formula! I don't. 'Trying our best with everything we got' is the best we can do at the time based on different influential factors such as emotional state, time, resources, skills, and other exposures. Not only in times of adversity, but in the moments of striving or climbing. The end result may not be in our favour, sometimes we get it right, other times wrong.

III
The battle of conflictual beliefs

A fox was moving slowly around the woods, in the search of food. He suddenly runs into a vineyard. As he gets closer, he begins to look closely and intensively at the grapes. Hmmm... delicious, my dinner! Floated in the air by a branch, grapes that never seemed more juicy, sweet, and colourful. The fox attempts to reach the grapes, realising that they were too high. He tries harder the second time, still no fruit. Feeling annoyed, he tries numerous times to leap into the air in different positions, but still not high enough. At the end, he stopped trying, placing his tail down, walking back in the woods revealing: "Why do I want grapes that are not even ripe yet? I don't want sour grapes." Because he couldn't get what he wanted, the fox ended up from the desire of wanting the grapes to an excuse that contradicted the first belief. The fox had 3 options to choose from:

1. Reaching the grapes in one or more attempts
2. Acknowledge that he wasn't capable enough to get the grapes
3. Create an excuse or a new thought which contradicted the first belief

Inspired from one of the Aesop's fables, this story applies to many of us, who cannot attain the intended desire, would voluntarily create then an additional belief of why the initial one was inappropriate. In a start-up business, when things don't perform as planned or desired, people often convince themselves that the business was destined to fail, attributing it

The battle of conflictual beliefs

to bad luck or time constraints. Phrases like, "I never had a real chance, I have had a bad intuition from the start, the economy is bad, there is too much competition," are repeatedly integrated into someone's thoughts. These contradictory beliefs can also manifest during an interview process where the candidate's nomination is unsuccessful. Instead of admitting that there were better candidates or they didn't prepare enough, an individual creates a conflicting narrative: "I wasn't treated fairly during the interview process. I didn't even like my potential boss, why do I bother to work for such a company?" In a romantic relationship there are no exceptions, especially during the early stages. When someone is interested in another person, have good intentions where the interaction doesn't go as expected, they might develop another belief such as. "I didn't really like him/her that much. He/she is boring." This is often concluded when there is no mutual agreement to meet again. However, there are times when, no matter how much we tried, prepared or how skillful we are, it's still not enough, where the job advertised was filled up by an internal candidate, or the business we believed would be successful from the beginning was unprofitable due to its geographical position and market evaluation. There are also occasions when these statements are valid, possibly the economy is bad, or the person was treated unfairly. Normally, the probability for this to happen is relatively low. Or perhaps, smarter than we think, the fox had a 4th option, realising that the grapes were far too high and unreachable, saving the remained energy and efforts for the next opportunity. Because it would be difficult to accept the situation at the time, which would cause discomfort, most of us tend to focus on the third option. How far can we go to cover up our own actions or thoughts? Sometimes, we do it in a way that becomes amusing. In most cases, choosing second option would be the most appropriate explanation, admitting to ourselves that we could be unskilled or unfit for the job, while we observe the opportunity to improve next time.

There are a few reasons why it can be extremely difficult to acknowledge that we are wrong at something. Firstly, nearly all of us tend to have a good opinion about ourselves, that we are doing the right thing, slightly kind-hearted, and quite quick-witted in some degree. When these beliefs are threatened, by admitting our mistakes, a defence mechanism may kick off automatically, protecting us. From what? Protecting us from our insecurities, doubts and discomfort! In this case, the mind is playing tricks with us. Secondly, we prefer not to consider that the problem lies within ourselves, breaking the architecture of our own thoughts and beliefs, reasoning that the other person was better, or we weren't skilled enough for the job. Instead, we develop a new belief stating that the initial desire was wrong anyway or finding an excuse elsewhere. In addition, if it happens without us even realising, how can we be certain that we are making the right choice? When two thoughts are in conflict simultaneously, we can ask ourselves: Is the new belief playing a part as an explanation because I can't reach the target or is it an attempt to rationalise the first one? With that in mind, if we can't admit when we are wrong at something from time to time in a specific scenario, we will miss out on opportunities for growth and self-improvement. It becomes challenging to become more rational with ourselves and others, especially when we get trapped in our stories, narratives of being right or that a problem lies elsewhere.

This phenomenon of cognitive dissonance was developed by Leon Festinger in 1957. His theory emphasised that when someone's ideas and thoughts are not in alignment with the desired action or outcome, it causes discomfort. To alleviate this comfort, a person's aim is to justify the error, effort or failure. With the aim of reducing their discomfort, this is usually achieved when an individual creates a new thought that contradicts the original one. Together with James Carlsmith, Festinger established and proved this theory in their psychological study presented in the book entitled 'A theory of cognitive dissonance'. In the experiment, approximately 70 participants were divided into two groups. Each group had the same task, to complete an uninteresting, repetitive and boring job. The aim of the exercise was to convince them that the boring job was actually enjoyable and interesting. The first group was paid $1 to lie about it, while the second group was offered 20$. After completing the task, participants were asked to rate their activity. At the end of the task, the second group had shown no exposure to cognitive dissonance, which was mainly driven by the higher incentive. They rated the task as less entertaining than initially aimed. In the 1st group, participants which received a much lower compensation, eventually began to believe the exercise they were doing was actually fun and interesting. In this experiment, Festinger described and anticipated that the 1st group which was paid $1 would find the task more enjoyable than those who were paid a higher amount. The underlying reason for this was highlighted due to no other justification for their participation in the activity. As a result, individuals with low or not enough motivation will convince themselves to improve any discomfort and avoid situations that are added as a contribution to their dissonance.

In consequence, the likelihood of falling under this cognitive error is particularly high in certain scenarios. We are all exposed to this phenomenon, especially when we hold two contradictory beliefs one after another. Scientists in the field of psychology argue that we mainly operate on two levels, the conscious and the unconscious. The conscious approach operates when we understand our own experiences when it comes to emotions, thoughts, memories and perceptions. In contrast, the unconscious mind works when any of those are activated in the background, behind the scenes, without our awareness. In addition, there is a preconscious level, which serves as a bridge between the two, when something can be easily brought into the conscious mind, information that can be easily recollected. For example, an individual forgets a name or something else but can recall it moments later. Many people believe that they function predominantly under the conscious level with full control on their decisions, while the research suggests otherwise. Many of our decisions are influenced by the unconscious mind. Sometimes, we might ask ourselves what is behind the surface or why we made a particular decision, and no further explanation can be found. Whether or not it was related to a threat, protection, danger, good feeling or past experience. One reason comes from the habits we are subjected to or have developed over the years. Another possible explanation arises from situations when something activates our emotions, thoughts, memories or various chemical messengers in the body. Almost everything we do on a daily basis, becomes a possibility to turn it into a habit, often without even realising it. Some of these habits can generate positive results in our lives and can be helpful such as exercising, maintaining a healthy diet, or writing down the priority list. There are also habits which are less beneficial like excessive drinking or being late all the time. As it might be expected, changing some of these habits can be quite challenging. It can take a considerable time until a habit is interrupted, stopped or replaced with a different one. In general, many of the habits formed in our early stages often shape the future results. A fictional character from 1843, Jacob Marley's ghost, illustrated this with the following statement, *"I wear the chains I forged in life"*. A chain that developed heavier and heavier with time and becoming unbreakable. The patterns he developed throughout his lifetime - centred around money and greed - created the fetters that shaped the chain he was holding.

One way to reduce the impact of unhelpful habits is to notice the dissonance. In normal times, we do have the tendency to rationalise it with another justification. Contradicting beliefs happen all the time, whether in our environment or personal matters, often slipping under our radar. There are insignificant errors, for example, when someone supports a healthy diet, but still engage in rich desserts by saying: "It's only an ice-cream, probably it doesn't even count." A more significant contradiction arises when an individual smokes, even though they are fully aware of the risks associated such as pulmonary disease or an increase in the biological age. I am not an exempt from this. Example of a justifying statement, *"There are people who smoked their entire life, and nothing happened!"* Individuals justify their dissonance or discomfort in various ways. For example, if the initial belief is "Excessive smoking is unhealthy", a reasonable approach is to acknowledge this belief and change the action. "Smoking is bad for my health, and in the upcoming days or weeks, I will come up with a plan to reduce or quit smoking". Excessive drinking or any example of this kind can be used. Below there are various approaches to rationalise the dissonance:

- Reasoning the conflictual thoughts: "I don't smoke that much anyway!"
- Justifying the initial thought with an extra one: "I will go for a run later, so it cancels out."
- Adding a new belief by denying the first one: "Smoking is not an actual problem; it helps me to get relaxed,

The battle of conflictual beliefs

they overestimate the effects. It's also good for social interactions where tasks are performed easier."

- Thinking about the consequences of quitting: "I will gain weight if I stop."
- Prolonging the discomfort: "I have plenty of time to do that. It's not that important now!"
- Accepting the interpersonal deception: "This is the only thing I do; I don't have any other."
- Keep postponing the belief by setting up a day: "From Monday onwards, I will stop smoking."
- Thinking about the process itself and the difficulty throughout: "There is no need to put myself under the strain of quitting."

Not acting when needed - Acting when not needed

Most of us are consciously aware that we need to exercise more, eat healthier, spend less than earning, practicing gratitude more frequently and so on. Yet again we don't do it often or not as much as we would like to. Partly because of dissonance. Another reason that underlines and sustains any of the postponed resolutions is known as the Akrasia effect – 'the state of acting is not in line with our own judgment'. In this case, the emotion is mixed up with the reason, leading to confusion.

It's Thursday evening, you're sitting comfortably and peacefully in your living room. It's been a busy and productive day and now you want to take some time as an opportunity to relax. From the beginning, you've been very clear to yourself. "I'll just watch an episode of my favourite series, before I go to sleep. Tomorrow, I need to wake up early to work on x activity." Few hours later: "Just one more episode, it's not that bad...!"

Four episodes later, the reasonable approach set initially has no sense anymore.

Below are different examples when emotions interfere with reasoning:

Not acting when needed

- Taking a few extra phone calls on a Friday afternoon to enhance performance and meet objectives, but choosing not to do so, probably feeling tired or already disconnected. Phrases like "I will look at it on Monday, or Why should I care when everybody else left the premises!" might arise.

- Considering applying for the same job role at a different company, which offers 20% salary increase and is closer to home, but still don't do it - partially due to comfort zone and security reasons, "I don't want to have to start from scratch again when it comes to the new environment, the people involved, and the processes, at least here I know how to handle things."

- Setting an alarm for early in the morning the night before with the intention of catching up on tasks and being productive but continually pressing the snooze button. Mainly because it feels good, and the emotion takes over the reasoning.

- Knowing the long-term benefits of adhering to a healthier diet but continuously postponing it. "I have time, I will do it next time, I just want to enjoy the moment."

- Understanding the effects of watching TV for longer than usual but still engaging in such scenario despite the awareness.

- Remaining in a comfort zone for too long, fully familiar of the negative consequences of such emotional state, but still failing to act.

Acting when not needed

- Getting angry when there is no need to do so, and even when you know entirely you shouldn't, but still getting wrapped up in such emotion.
- Staying late with your friends despite knowing that you have responsibilities early the next day, which may alter the effectiveness of those by doing so.
- Engaging in a dishonest behaviour even though you are fully aware of the consequences from the very beginning and then attempting to justify it with different explanations.
- After a break-up decision, you may find yourself second-guessing, switching your mind up and realising that it may not have been the best choice.
- Indulging in short-term pleasures like gambling or substance use, despite being fully aware of the negative consequences associated with those.
- Establishing a start-up company even when the actual research doesn't recommend to do so based on the initial criteria and historical key performance indicators that outline a potential good acquisition, but still do it.
- Choosing an investment decision even when the price of the investment sale is too high in relation to what it's worth, partly believing of missing a great opportunity compared to the past performance.

In consequence, we are all exposed to some of these activities from time to time, the actual outcome depends on how often they are initiated. The dissonance effect may show up differently in someone's behaviour when it comes to working environment. For example, individuals may resort to blame, deception or aggression to reduce the discomfort of their own contradictory beliefs. In addition, when someone believes they are in the wrong job as well as finding the company's procedures unethical, they continue to be there for financial reasons, even when the conflictual beliefs are present. The dissonance effect can lead further to high inconsistency and indecisiveness when engaging in unpleasant activities. It prompts people to switch their thoughts and beliefs to lower the pain. One way to minimise the effect is to understand what you experience. Simply, to become consciously aware of your own emotional state. Another important aspect is to change the behaviour or action as well as the individual perspectives. Changing a belief can be a challenging task to translate it into practice, as we have done it so many times before. It requires a high cognitive effort from the individual to switch or alter the initial beliefs.

From time to time, regardless of how much we try to avoid or reduce the dissonance, it's just not possible. It comes with life's opportunities and decisions we are exposed to regularly. For instance, when someone is offered a job opportunity in a different part of the world, surrounded by beautiful places and glamorous attractions. If not, they could be driven by a separate incentive. In one way or another, they will experience dissonance, regardless of whether the individual refuses or accepts the offer. In case of declining the offer, they may reflect on the experiences they could have missed and losing the opportunity to be nearer the desired place. On the contrary side, they might find themselves missing their close family members and friends. For this reason, acceptance can be a wonderful thing, where you can embrace both old and new ideas, the negatives or positives for each case, regardless of the outcome.

Another applicable example arises when we're exposed to a choice at the crossroads, whether professionally or academically. If you decided to study law, you can't study at the same time another subject, for example, finance. In other words, an opportunity is missed out regardless of the chosen domain. The effect becomes stronger if after several years the chosen field does not work favourably to your side, finding another field of attraction, or shifting the attention to a new area of expertise. Nonetheless, there are situations at hand, where dissonance can help us. For example, when someone dislikes something, based on their personal preferences and yet they take the right actions towards it. You may not like certain activities such as exercising or reading half an hour each day, but these actions contribute to a healthier life, as research shows. Dissonance can be also advantageous when it allows a person to move on, without being stuck on a simple idea or concept for too long. For the clever fox, even by admitting the grapes were unripe, was a way to move on to find a different alternative.

IV
Emotional equilibrium - the golden ratio

Did you know that we spend more time with ourselves than with anyone else? Every day we experience tens of thousands of emotions, feelings, sensations and thoughts combined from the moment we wake up until we go to sleep. We do it approximately every second of the wakeful time. This combination is expressed throughout the day, consciously or subconsciously, depending on the situation we are in. Whether we are optimistic, disappointed, annoyed, hungry, dynamic, tired or calm, emotions represent a critical role in our daily life. Additionally, thoughts that are expressed continuously in our mind: "I don't like my new colleague, I feel I am doing too much and not getting the reward needed, I'm wondering what I should have for dinner tonight, the economy is going to soar or plummet any time from today, this person chats nonsense, I might be in the wrong profession, I just need to be patient - the result will come, it's only Wednesday today - but it feels like Thursday, this change represents a good opportunity now, I wish I go back in time and change a few things, I better book that vacation as it might get unavailable or too expensive." This mixture of senses can help us to live at our best and ultimately take better decisions to improve ourselves. But that's not always the case, at the same time it can make us inadequate to think and act clearly, to be more rational with ourselves and with those around.

Everything we do in our lives, starts from our internal state, the way how we interact with ourselves and the outside world. The pulse suddenly changes, the blood pressure may rise or fall, where some of the bodily hormones such as adrenaline or dopamine may get activated. These responses including facial expressions and other physiological changes in our body, serve like transmitters as a source of information, helping to maintain the equilibrium of homeostasis and ultimately how we respond when facing various scenarios. These reactions are emotions. They are processed in real time to enable timely decision-making and responsiveness. A feeling, instead, is an awareness in our mind when we experience those emotions. Emotions take place all the time but not always we experience a sense of feeling.

Fear, a valuable emotion we possess, saves our life numerous times protecting us from danger. When approached by a deadly animal or any other life-threatening condition, the fear initiates alertness, which creates a simplified solution in our brain of how we respond to such conditions. The clever thinking will not help us. "Is it friendly, is it playful, is it lost?" Similarly, when we cross a road and observe a car approaching at a high speed. During the alertness time, which happens extremely fast, some of the brain functions will switch off creating only 2 binary responses, known as the flight or fight responses. Sometimes, a 3rd mode is activated, the freezing mode. This response is induced involuntarily and automatically, to help and protect us, in this specific case stopping the deadly animal from perceiving any motion. At the same time, in less severe scenarios, fear can prevent us from pursuing our personal aspirations. In other words, holding us back. This fear may be attributed in different ways, one being the fear of failure. In such event, the irrational emotion will make us ineffective acting like a barrier to move towards the path we want. "I fear to do x, so I will not do it." The fear of rejection is another pervasive feeling, but present in our lives, where we might jump to conclusion too soon, thinking about the worst-case scenario in a given situation. In both cases, we anticipate experiencing unpleasant and difficult emotions, and we want to avoid them. This approach of thinking will make us ineffective and unable to attempt even trying. When we encounter such emotions or thoughts from time to time, it's important to cultivate emotional courage. In other words, despite being aware of the fear, developing various actions to overcome it while confronting the unpleasant state. The thinking process that we adopted initially might help us, on the basis that we become aware of it. On one hand it can hinder us, on the other it can help us. If an exam or job interview is scheduled next week, and you feel nervous, worried, or fearful, that's not necessarily a bad thing. It means preparation and effort may be required. When considering the worst-case scenarios, by reframing the initial thought into a question: What is actually the worst thing that can happen? We tend to realise that is not as bad as we initially thought it was. Of course, with that in mind, we should not forget that periodically the reality is different from the one in our mind. Since we haven't become emotionally attached, or related to that experience, we may win a professional sport game outside the lounge, come up with the most creative solutions after an event or beforehand, give the most well-intentioned opinions from an external point of view, but when we find ourselves in that situation - things may be slightly slippery, or in other words there is room for improvement.

There are times when the biggest fears or worries can eventually transform into the biggest strengths or assets over time. One noteworthy example is the experience of Jim Kwik. Born in July 1973, he spent most of his childhood in school having difficulties of learning and memorising. For a decade and a half, due to a head injury he had in kindergarten, he was not able to keep up with the other students in the learning experience, despite the extra time and effort he was making continuously to catch up. This caused him to experience significant challenges and difficulties, that affected his personal life, becoming continuously worried and withdrawn from others. As a result, at the age of 18, he considered quitting school, as the challenge of keeping up with it became too intense in the learning experience. During the first semester's break, along with his family, visited a family friend in the surroundings of California. While there, his father's friend asked him several questions: "How's school? Why are you in school? What are your dreams?" A blank paper was handed to him to write the answers down. After writing his dreams, Jim father's friend looked back at him, revealing: "Jim, you are so close to achieving all these dreams," while illustrating a small gap between his hands (approximately 8-10 inches). Jim replied, "There is no way I can do this, give me 10 lifetimes and I still won't not be able to achieve this." In response, his father's friend moved his hands up in line with his head. In other words, referring to his mind. Later, this family friend became his mentor. Not long after, Jim Kwik began to turn the page upside down, changing his way of thinking, reflecting on himself, why he had troubles with learning and memorising. He focused primarily on his biggest weaknesses - finding it extremely difficult to learn and being a slow learner. As a result of that, he asked himself if there was a way how to learn faster. Over the next years, he focused entirely on different activities and programmes aimed to improve how to learn and memorise, rather than focusing on what to learn. A few decades later, he became one of the world's brightest minds, a brain coach, and the co-founder of Kwik learning. He also is author of 'Limitless', a New York Times bestselling book. After overcoming his childhood struggles with learning, he is now able to teach people around the world, including those from the largest companies such as Google, World Press or Harvard

University. The aim is entirely based on memory improvement, how to learn faster and more effectively.

When considering the extreme emotion such as excitement, the bodily symptoms resemble those of fear. Both can result in accelerated heart rate, increased alertness, and a change in the breathing process. With similar physiological symptoms, the difference is not how the body responds, but instead how the brain understands and translates it. Imagine having this wrong, to get excited when you meant to be fearful. Some of these extreme emotions are commonly experienced in our lives, where one cannot be triggered without the other. There is also a fine line between them. It may not take much time or effort to shift from one to another. Example: laughing - crying, happiness - sadness, love - hate, hardworking - indolence, agility - rigidity, effectiveness - ineffectiveness, perseverance - procrastination. When one intensifies at one end, the more exposed we are on the opposite side of the other emotion. This concept is identified as opponent process theory. When experiencing an emotion to a high end, shortly after, the opposite emotion is triggered to compensate the first reaction. For example, experiencing a high degree of happiness and enjoyment over the weekend, a person may express a slight melancholic emotional state thereafter. At the same time, they display a symmetry that is intensified proportionally. For example, the more tired we get, the better the relaxation is. Water never tastes better than after running 5 miles in a hot weather condition. Happiness feels greater when we go through difficult moments or handle various challenges. In other words, the harder the pain, the greater the reward. Similarly, the more we love or value something, the more exposed we are to discomfort and pain. The intensity level increases or decreases depending on the situation at hand and how much effort was allocated initially. This is a way to compensate our emotions, normally the extreme emotions we hold and experience, particularly the ones with a higher impact.

In the summer of 2023, I went back to my hometown to visit my family. It was an ordinary vacation. Surprisingly, in a good way, I met my cousin, whom I hadn't seen in 15 years. He kindly invited me to his house for lunch, which was a nice gesture. During our conversation, I noticed that he was living in a 10-bedroom house, with a spacious lounge and other amenities. This was quite unusual for me and surprising at the same time. Shortly before leaving, I couldn't help but ask him, "I hope you don't mind my asking, why the choice of your house since you have only one child, and all the other rooms are probably unoccupied?" "Good question," he replied. "Now, I shall answer! When I was a child, up to my teenage years, you probably remember, I had to share the same room, even a bed, with my two other brothers as we didn't have a room allocated for each of us. The situation was difficult, my parents tried their best to provide but still it was not adequate. It was a difficult period at the time, with not many full-time jobs available nearby. So I've decided, due to the lack of privacy, when I become an adult, I would never want to have this problem again. It's a bit silly I know; I don't need all of them, the extra rooms are costly and need to be maintained. As a result, the additional rooms are just a reflection from what happened in the past, nothing else, trying to avoid the previous scenario." Because of his strong emotions from the past, my cousin tried to compensate those moments by remembering the impactful stories from his teenage years.

Then I arrived in the UK, I met my friend for catching up. In his house, I noticed an abundance of a specific fruit in the kitchen and living room. It was not unnoticeable. The fruit wasn't something unusual, as it can easily be found in every grocery shop and probably household. I said: "I didn't know you liked this fruit so much!" He replied: "When I was little, growing up in an impoverished area, this fruit was extremely expensive at the time and unaffordable for most people, while I didn't have access to such 'treat'. So I thought when I get older, I didn't want to be exposed to a situation reminding me of those times. Surprisingly, I only taste it occasionally now."

We all probably experienced a similar situation to a certain degree. Even though it might not be useful for us at the time, but instead recalling the emotions that were affected by past events. Emotional compensation is a way of balancing these emotions and feelings. It represents a *recompense* in relation to the unpleasant and painful moments from different times related. This compensation can manifest in various ways relatively from the previous times, where someone seeks and adopts different ways to feel better about themselves or to avoid similar scenarios in the future. These ways can be diversified from *physical comfort* - acquiring extra material possessions, either as a distraction or substitution, *relationships* - overprotective parent or partner, *academic* - emphasising too much on this aspect to cover different areas of failure and neglect everything else. In essence, these responses aim to address emotional imbalance. Helping others is another form to reward the feelings of shame or guilt. Throughout modern history, various people have displayed this type of behaviour, as they showed something immoral or dangerous, they tried to display the opposite emotions. At the same time, it plays an important role as it encourages growth, improvement and resilience.

There are up to 34,000 emotions available we can experience according to the psychologist Robert Plutchik and other studies. Most of them are grouped in clusters, often described by similarities and small differences in intensity. For example, with regard to the intensity related to anger, we might experience a range of emotions such as touchy, irritated, displeased, annoyed, upset, agitated, resentful, outraged, furious, despaired.

However, there are 8 fundamental emotions that we commonly experience: joy, fear, anger, sadness, surprise, disgust, trust and anticipation. From these primary emotions can be extended the secondary ones such as confusion, jealousy, optimism, love, frustration, shame, vulnerability, guilt, content and so on. Yet, we are more likely to experience negative emotions rather than positive ones. This is because we are more open to different threats than opportunities. Dr Robert Scharf, a professor in applied linguistics, describes that from all the emotions in our vocabulary, the negatives ones represent 50%, positives 30%, and neutral the remaining percentage. When experiencing negative feelings, they involve slightly additional thinking and explanation when compared to the positive ones. Despite the threat conditions, once we feel the positive ones, we become rapidly aware and partially conscious that we are safe, and no further actions or engagements are necessary. In this context, media and advertisements companies often distribute more stories with greater emotional impact negatively, to grab the attention of users and readers. There are also emotions available that are encountered but hard to explain. For example, monachopsis, nodus Tollens, Schadenfreude, sonder, a 'veiled' joy, ambivalence. Sometimes, a profound association when it comes to these emotions is identified as ineffable, beyond words. E.g. a 'veiled joy'. A parent may feel this bittersweet emotion when one of their children finishes high school with a good grade and prepare to leave home to follow their further interest. A mixture of emotions can be sensed at the same time, such as happiness and sadness.

Using negative words or sentences doesn't necessarily mean we are open for a gloomy and pessimistic mindset, but instead they can add meaning to a sentence. E.g. "If you *don't* wash your hands, you will get diseases!" It basically translates into "Wash your hands!". Now, the same sentence without "don't", "If you wash your hands, you will get diseases!" However, while this sentence doesn't guarantee the outcome either way, it suggests a higher probability of a disease if hands are not washed. Consider the following, "I feel bad" vs "I *don't* feel bad". The first sentence is considered negative, while the second a positive one, due to an added word. "Are you looking forward to your vacation?" Reply: "I *can't* wait for it!" In this case, the negative word gives the sentence context, to be excited about something, rather than being attained by the lack of patience. Double negatives can also be used for optimism or affirmation: "I *cannot not* go!", which means "I will certainly go!" Beyond our environment and what we see around, from building architectures, engineering to high advance technologies, (e.g. automotive, aerospace, railway, food manufacturing, etc), the development stage of new products or facilities starts with the following key question for each element - "*What can go wrong?*" This methodological approach is not only a powerful tool to identify all the potential failures during the planning stage and what the reality may bring at the time, but also represents a valuable technique to create and set up new methods, more sustainable solutions to avoid, prevent or reduce such failures that are identified at the early stage. For instance, designing a new storey apartment building in the planning phase: *What can go wrong?* In one case amongst many others, the building can catch fire. How to prevent or minimise such risk? – using anti-inflammatory materials, integrating safety procedures for people and emergency exit routes, adding fire detectors and alarm in place, incorporating automatic sprinklers to switch off the fire and so on.

When you drive on a highway and hear a lousy, irritating noise from your tyres or engine bay, you stop safely, check it and try to fix the issue immediately. This is the way you know something is wrong. It would be a problem if you had a fault and didn't hear the noise, becoming unsafe and dangerous. Normally, no matter how tired, hungry or worried you are, that won't stop you taking the necessary actions to address the issue. Similarly, when it comes to our emotions, feelings of being suppressed, concerned, or frustrated, might indicate that something deeper is going on. When becoming aware of those, perhaps, an action is necessary. This could create some discomfort at the time, thoughts like, "Ohhh no, not now! I must spend more time, effort and money." But at the same time, we should be thankful due to their warning system. Dealing with disappointment can tells us about something we care that didn't go according to plan. Next time, either reducing the expectations from a particular event or aligning them closely with the reality we live in. Similarly, feeling frustrated might arise from experiencing an unfair treatment, witnessing injustice amongst our peers, something important to us was threatened or we did something unethical against our own morals.

Painful emotions (e.g. shame, regret, guilt) are not necessarily considered "bad". The same can be said for pleasant emotions. Feeling happy, relaxed or comfortable for too long comes with its own negative effects. When we are happy, we don't want to change something, why would we? We want to stop the time at that moment, and that will not allow us to engage, nor to attempt in challenges or any difficult scenarios to improve ourselves, especially when the reality may bring different unexpected scenarios from time to time. On a different note, there is no real contrast to compare our happiness with. When experiencing it for too long, becoming the new normal, how do I know if I am happy if I'm continuously happy? Alternatively, if painful emotions persist for longer than normal, they will bring their own effects, feeling stressful when there is no need, we may find it difficult to prosper. The clear, rational point of view is hard to find, and they can only extend the discomfort or pain, avoiding living our life in a way that ignores both the good and the bad, not as from our imagination; flowery and rosy, or cloudy and gloomy.

As life is inevitable to changes, changes of any kind, good or bad in every aspect of life, how should we show up to our emotions when we encounter them? Susan David, a PhD, in the medical school at Harvard University and the author of *Emotional Agility*' describes that emotions are data not directives, they represent valuable information to us and we should not act as if they are fixed concepts or stones, but instead embrace them and understand what they are trying to tell us. They are often represented as functions to help the individual. She indicates how we should show up to them, with love, gentle acceptance, and curiosity. Susan spent her interest in the field of emotions for more than 2 decades. She emphasised that, in normal circumstances, there are two main ways how an individual approaches their own emotions:

- *The bottling-way.* When we mostly tend to ignore our emotions and put them to one side e.g. "It's not a good time to think about this right now." "My partner has called to invite me to a dinner at the in-laws, which I don't want," "I don't want to deal with this situation now, I will do that later." Individuals may be exposed to a different thinking such as: "Everything will be fine, why worry," "Don't waste time, just do it", neglecting any information related to the subject at hand. This to avoid the inner conflict we might find ourselves with. In other words, aiming to postpone the actual feelings.

- *The brooding way*. This involves constantly thinking about a recent scenario in comparison to how we meant to think or feel in that time; it can become an overthinking and overwhelming process based on a continuous thinking cycle making the worst of ambiguity. "I shouldn't feel the way I feel!" Basically, we use thinking as a tool at a high frequency, of what we were supposed to feel in a closed loop.

Due to these factors, when both ways are used at a high intensity, individuals are often confronted with small irritation points that built over time and eventually come out sooner or later. E.g. It's Wednesday evening. You've had a reasonable day and are looking forward to some relaxation before the night begins. You sit quietly in the living room, perhaps watching TV or just reading a book. Suddenly, your partner starts engaging with you, shifting the conversation, for no reason whatsoever, bringing back memories from six months ago, and not in a nostalgic way. You may wonder, where did that come from? Why do they act like that? You may think they lost the plot…! Other common examples include when walking out from a customer meeting, regardless of the subject and its intensity. Or someone suddenly says or does something related to an 'unexplained' behaviour, it's most likely not because of what happened at the time, but from 'unresolved issues' that occurred while ago and using that causation to manifest a different one. The cognitive energy and high intensity are built up over time, waiting to be expressed or surface. This normally reflects how we interact with our own emotions and thoughts.

Both ways explored at high frequency are disadvantageous to our emotional wellbeing over time, since they demand a cognitive resource, deliberately or not, related to our internal feelings and thoughts. We all experience them from time to time, that's why it's important to adopt an equilibrium. A sense of balance within our emotional tolerance, what is possible or not, able to experience, learn and embrace the full spectrum of emotions from low to high intensity. Appreciating and understanding comfort, often comes from enduring hard work, facing challenges and overcoming difficult times. When it comes to 'simplicity' in a cognitive way, adhering to 'thinking dissection' from time to time can be a good idea.

Thinking has an influence on our feelings, and feelings on our thinking. The complex and dynamic relationship between the two, I would call it 'the marriage'. Where one person's actions affect the other and vice versa, working together and one for another to share a common goal. Our thoughts have the power to trigger emotions, which in turn shape our feelings. When we become aware of this process, we can better understand and manage our emotional responses. In addition, feelings influence the thinking process and ultimately the decisions we make. E.g. "My neighbour keeps parking up in the front of my drive, I'd better have a word with them, nicely and politely." Research shows that feelings are the predominant factor between the two. When certain emotions are activated, our initial reactions might be automatic, but our subsequent thoughts can alter the way we feel about the situation. The mind aims to find sensible answers to the way we feel, while manifesting those feelings through thinking. When feeling relaxed, peaceful, in harmony, the way we think is different as we are more open to ideas, creativity or dealing with challenges in a different manner. In contrast, when we are resentful or filled with hate, the ability to think clearly might be absent, only focusing on one side of the information and that's often not the appropriate one.

There are different levels of thinking approaches available to us, some of which we may not even be aware of. They vary from low to high intensity when it comes to complexity. For example, from comprehension to evaluation, metacognition to inference. Below are highlighted some of the basic ones, especially those that are harmonised with feelings.

The feeling vs thinking relationship, or the 'marriage' can cause instantaneous reactions. Some of these approaches used in our daily routine are programmed and identified as reflexes. For example, when we hear a baby crying, unscrew a bottle cap when we feel thirsty, hear some bad news on TV, or someone jumps to the front of the queue. Some of these reactions are natural responses derived from our values, morals, or environment. They are sometimes considered beneficial for human survival. Simply, taking a decision in no time with no need to engage in a cognitive effort. Every so often, we are engaged in those responses, because we have repeated them numerous times and eventually they become a natural habit. Drinking coffee in the morning, shopping when feeling bored, calling the loved one at some intervals, are additional examples. Yet, on a different spectrum, these automatic responses might not be appropriate, making us blinded and acting on a state of impulse. "You lied to me first, I only returned the favour!" This is where we can jumble everything up, where no room for additional thinking is left. Perhaps asking yourself: Is that really important? Rather than acting on the immediate feeling. Self-awareness comes into its role in helping us acknowledge what we feel and most likely change something if necessary.

Now, we can move to 'yes' and 'no' decisions. These usually arise during times of high alertness, fear or similar situations. In other words, a simplified answer, one way or the other. This approach also applies in a normal situation that requires a simple answer. For example: Will you join the dinner tonight? Are you hungry? Do you want to travel tomorrow?

Careful thinking is more grounded on elaborated thinking, for example: choosing your professional career, the place you decide to live without the job's incentive, or buying a property based on location, no. of bedrooms, style, neighbourhood, amenities, financial growth and so on.

During this process, a person considers taking actions related to an important area of their life, which can evoke feelings that require further contemplation. Individuals often cling to certain thoughts based on the emotions they wish to experience.

Detailed thinking involves a process that occurs during something complicated, a problem solving, a novel. This type of thinking can be employed to estimate something based on unknown information, which can lead to new ideas where a person wasn't aware from the start. In this process lies the attention to the tiniest details and lateral thinking. Many difficult problems are resolved through this cognitive method. At the same time, it's important to recognise what this type of thinking can do on a regular basis when there is no need for it, resulting in additional effort, complexity, difficulty, tension and sometimes misery. Misery, more in a hesitant and unrelaxed way, spending too much time when it comes to make a quick decision. Alternatively, if a situation requires attention to details, when attention to details is the most needed, it can intensify a problem to become fuzzier, often losing sight of the whole picture, the entire perspective. E.g., someone pays attention to too many details using pros and cons for each alternative, as a result they are unable to observe the most influential factors related to the subject.

Depending on the situation at hand, we will need all of them on a regular basis, switching on and off between those to a point when one no longer serves us. Mostly everything can be mixed up here. If detailed thinking is used for something that requires simplicity, it often brings unwanted problems and challenges; for example: selecting a meal or a holiday destination. A good way is to distinguish the time when we should use it. Switching on and off between those scenarios can be extremely important and valuable to achieve growth. Whenever a situation requires a different type of thinking, it comes to our perception to acknowledge the mode we are currently in.

The waves

When you are full of frustration, raising the voice and participating in different violent activities, you are not thinking and consciously gone. The emotion takes you over completely, so that you are becoming the anger in that time. You are not considering: Why am I behaving like that? Am I doing the right thing? Few moments later, probably the emotion has gone. Hopefully, before a real damage was left behind. Driven by impulse and the lack of awareness, many of the immoral and bad acts occur during these moments. Different studies show that our emotions last approximately 90 seconds before starting to dissipate, which reflect a temporary reaction inside our bodily system. Dr Joan Rosenberg, an American psychologist expands this information in more detail in the book entitled '90 Seconds to a Life you Love'. Not long after, an individual has more influence to choose and influence their internal behaviour. Some people describe emotions like 'ocean waves' where they 'come and go', and trying to stop them might not be the best solution. Due to their complexity and intensity, different approaches are applicable for certain scenarios as there is no golden rule for how we should handle them every single time. Almost every emotion has its own pros and cons: For example, 'crying' is often associated with a distressful, painful and sad experience. It's also considered a relief, working as a recovery response to restore the emotional balance. Furthermore, crying releases endorphins, which can improve the person's mood, as long as it's done on a genuine basis. At the same time, this is observed when experiencing an elevated level of happiness during an empathetic response or a pleasant surprise. Most of the times, 'laughing' is attributed to happiness, humour and during the feel-good moments. Sometimes, this behaviour can appear as a denial mode, creating a masking effect when something is wrong. In some cases, a "smiling depression" is associated where someone pretends to be okay and hides their true emotions to avoid causing harm, worries, or any burdens to their loved ones.

Other examples:

Avoidance

- stops harmful situations, conflict and any other dangerous scenarios when there is no need
- missing different life opportunities, lack of flexibility, limited choices over time

Persistency

- improves the likelihood to complete goals and tasks, promotes motivation, personal growth and resilience
- reduces flexibility, focusing on only one thing and ignoring anything else leading to obsession, the costs associated with its implications can be higher, excessive tension affecting the individual's wellbeing

Tidiness

- brings order in place, increases productivity, objects are found easily
- reduces creativity, flexibility, and innovation

Procrastination

- allows more time in case some something was overlooked or discounted, potentially improving the end goal efficiency, switching to different tasks in between, requires less time to finish something due to the full engagement
- brings feelings of inferiority, putting things off, a task may never start off, interest is no longer present, reduces performance and efficiency, running out of time to complete the task

Some of the most fascinating things in nature and human body are represented by a ratio, how a part is related to another. Known as the golden ratio, the number is represented by the Greek letter 'phi', which is equivalent to approximately 1.618.... This number with unique properties was discovered and found in the early years of 500BC, by the Greek mathematicians Pythagoras and Euclid of Alexandria. From the 13th century onwards, it gained further attention through the work of several scientists such as Fibonacci, Nicolas Bernoulli, and Leonard Euler. This golden ratio is found in the universe, surrounding flora, environment and throughout objects, art or creative silhouettes. Sometimes, illustrated through a spiral, it can originate from flowers to animals and human beings. This ratio can be observed further in renowned masterpieces such as Monalisa and Parthenon Marble.

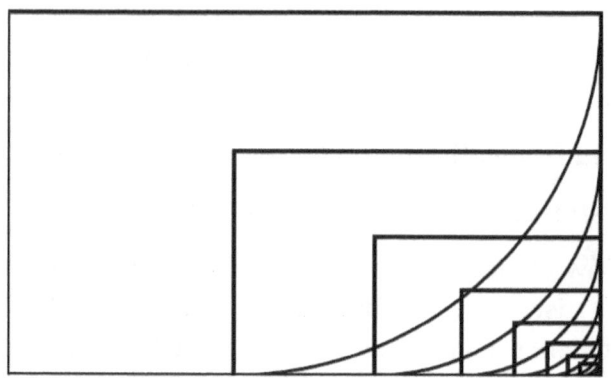

Example of golden ratio through a series of rectangles and a spiral

To give us a more balanced life, a projection, can the human emotions be also represented by this ratio? To round it up, 62% positives and 38% negatives. In other words, the frequency of usage between the 2. The neutral emotions are disregarded in this context, but they play a part too in relation to any of those. If they represented around 20% of the total emotions, the ratio would then change to 52% and respectively 28%. However, there is not enough data and analysis related to this subject. This is just an ordinary example.

According to University of North Carolina Research, the current ratio is 3 to 1; for every negative feeling or thought we should have 3 positive ones to achieve growth. This means 75% positives with the remaining negatives. The golden ratio is slightly more accurate, where the reality of our emotional experiences depends on so many factors such as genetic background, personal traits, environmental exposure, chance, age and significant life events (e.g. wedding, exams, marriage, birth, etc). Human emotions may not be quantifiable by a mathematical ratio. When it comes to this positive vs negative ratio, there will be moments or chapters in our lives where we might experience 10 to 1, 3 to 1, 1 to 10, or 1 to 1. During various events such as divorce, losing a loved one, anniversaries or vacations, this ratio is highly dependent on such events. During difficult times, showing a positive ratio of 10 to 1, there is something 'wrong' I suppose, only if the manifestation of the feeling is not authentic.

V
The error of confirmation

You have listened to your favourite artist lately and probably don't like it. You had the intention to purchase a car from your preferred automaker and noticed that you are slightly disappointed by the latest models released. Why do we like a certain artist or car brand? Or why do we agree or disagree with a particular sport, profession or religion?

Two old friends, John and Jack, are meeting after a while in a café bar. Somehow, they brought up one of the points of discussion, the existence of God. Since they have known each other for a long time, they have completely different perspectives when it comes to the existence of God. John is a priest in the local community, while Jack is a physician, and he is an outsider of this belief. Jack reveals first: "Look, I have been trying several times, it simply wasn't effective!" John replies with some amazement: "When is the last time you prayed? Did you do it truthfully from the heart?" "It was actually not long ago," Jack says. "I was recently on a trip in a seasonal mountain snow resort. I was away from the main place, as I wanted to explore the surroundings and close vicinity. Meanwhile, a horrible snowstorm arrived. I was lost, the temperature reached below -20 degrees, surrounded by high wind and not able to see anything around me. I was feeling hopeless, and helpless at that time. Therefore, I tried to pray on to my knees: If there is a God, as I am in the middle of this blizzard, please help me, otherwise I am not going to make it alive." John looks in his friend's eyes and replies: "After this experience, it's a miracle that you are here with me, you must believe in God now after all!" Jack surprisingly responds: "No, no, this is not what happened! A few people were passing by and helped me find the way to the camp." John had nothing further to say. Why do such different beliefs occur and where do they come from? Social beliefs and values are normally adopted on from generation to generation and ultimately from the living environment. John understood from his family that God is behind everything, while Jack was raised in a family that considered only scientific knowledge.

If the artist didn't lose their abilities, or the car manufacturer its innovative attributes, what could be the cause? Well, the reason why we love music or a specific car brand, is based on anticipation, resonance, and perception. When the artist shifts their style, they fail to satisfy our expectations. Similarly in the case of car manufacturer, when it changes its design architecture. Surprisingly, our mind is not processing the music in that manner but in addition intends to seek patterns and connections in almost everything we do, see, or absorb. This information created develops our perceptions and beliefs, the way we understand and interpret something. Once a belief is formed, we try further and search for additional supportive information, to pacify ourselves by not disrupting the beliefs we hold. We find confirmation in the news, society, from our past or what others tell us. While this search for information can be effective, it has also a downside, as we tend to agree and confirm something associated with our own beliefs and any other ideas we tend to ignore even when we might find evidence against them. Vice versa is applicable too when we disagree with something. Any material that endangers the architecture of our own beliefs and perceptions will be ignored. We simply dislike when a pattern or model is interrupted, it chooses to continue listening to that pleasant music. If different, it generates discomfort, disappointment, and irritation especially when feelings and habits are present. Often, we are continuously searching for reassurance of our pre-conclusions, expectations, and beliefs. This phenomenon is called *confirmation bias.*

Whenever we encounter a situation or fact related to a subject, we often look at those by either amplifying or simplifying our perspective. None of us is except from this tendency. This occurrence is identified as one of the most hidden errors we are exposed to. Critical and logical thinking is often exhausting, especially in a fast-paced environment, where we frequently need to depend on our own abilities or instincts to make quick decisions. If we acknowledge that we are wrong at something, we should also challenge the fact that we don't think as rationally as we think we are. This process helps us to become more aware of our own tendencies and showing that some situations are often more complex than we initially thought. A renowned psychologist Daniel Kahneman said: *"A reliable way to make people believe in falsehoods is frequent repetition. Because familiarity is not easily distinguished from the truth,"* which suggests if there is time to reflect, most likely tends to be a reasonable idea.

Confirmation bias implies the following effects:

- Attitude polarisation. In this case, the individual's beliefs become stronger, and the argument develops more intense even when an evidence is presented.

- Belief persistence. It's the ability of people to hold on to their initial beliefs even when the new information and evidence contradicts that belief.

- Illusionary correlation. This effect occurs when a person 'sees' and 'believes' a relationship based on the 2 variables that are not associated with each other nor do exist.

- Wishful thinking. It focuses on the creation of beliefs of what we want to see and imagine rather than the evidence or reality.

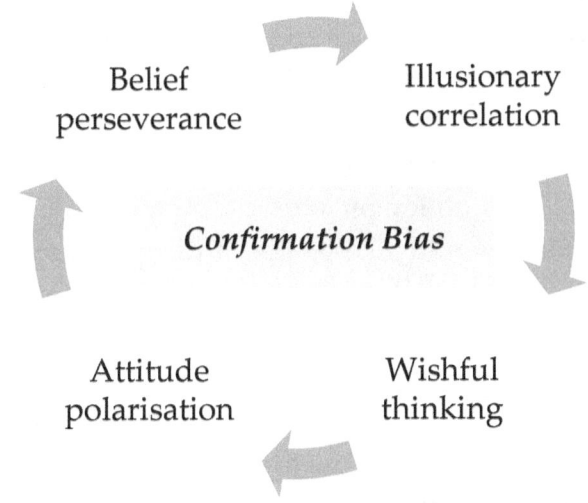

Self-awareness is one of the key ingredients to get out of the circle. When exposed to this phenomenon, what can be done in this situation? Confirmation bias is not easy to overcome, to some extent it cannot be eliminated from our lives. Nobody likes to acknowledge when they are wrong or being criticised, instead continuously seeking proof that their story is the right one. Once we form an idea or perception, it can be extremely challenging to change it. To further extend this concept, the error of confirmation turns out sometimes to what is often referred to as the man with the hammer syndrome. More explicitly, "To the man with the hammer, every problem looks like a nail." The man gets really attached and in love with his hammer. He will treat every problem like a nail and neglect anything else. He uses the hammer, even for a more obvious scenario, when dealing with a screw and there is a screwdriver available next to. He finds it extremely challenging to change his beloved tool. He used the hammer in the past and probably worked effectively on a few occasions. It doesn't necessarily mean it works the same next time. This thinking approach is one of the Abraham

Maslow's trademarks amongst other people throughout modern history. It was later supported by Charlie Munger in 1994. Charlie Munger is recognised for his worldly wisdom, what he encountered through his life experience and through different activities as a vice-president of Berkshire Hathaway. Unfortunately, he is no longer with us. He passed away in 2023, at the age of 99. I would like to take this opportunity to thank him for his contributions to society and for sharing the learning experiences with the outside world. The idea behind the hammer concept can be extended further to different disciplines, where a person approaches all the possible challenges and problems with the same solution. For example, a marketing department focuses only on marketing strategies, not paying attention to the quality of product or anything else. From an architect's point of view, problems are approached in real life to the guidelines specific in their discipline. For every encountered scenario, we should consider ourselves as the man with a toolbox. In this case, every idea or concept represents a tool, before facing a challenge, where a tool can be switched on and off or adding new ones too. Perhaps even replacing or eliminating the old ones if they no longer serve us or become rusty. This is not straightforward as it might seem to alternate between different ideas, because the mind tries to reject immediately the new ways due to the most valuable beliefs we hold. These beliefs are different from person to person. Adopting a new idea might represent a challenging task, especially if the old ones have been in use for too long, or if the new ones have not been tested before, which enables uncertainty. Even more primarily when people aim for certainty or safety.

Confirmation bias comes in various forms. For example, we support someone who is skilled or famous in some specific domain because it matches our own belief system, but if the same information is provided by someone we don't know or less competent, we tend to disregard it. In other words, we use association only attributed to someone competent and knowledgeable to confirm our own beliefs. In this context, I believe that this is not the most appropriate thinking approach we may hold. In addition, we tend to agree with others in the presence of doubt, even though considering that the information proposed could be incorrectly or falsely associated.

Emily has a strong belief that left-handed people are more creative than those who are right-handed. Whenever Emily meets someone who is left-handed, she assigns greater significance to this information, since it supports her initial belief. She then further cherry-picks any additional information that her assumptions to remain unchanged. She ignores any evidence that contradicts her belief.

Amy, on the other hand, claims that people who are born as Gemini are often easy going, communicative, creative along with other features. When a sign of Gemini's features is shared through a horoscope, she will then support that information to a much larger extent, even though there is no correlation between the two, research indicates - between the personality features and astrological signs. For example, "This month, you will meet someone that has a big influence in your life, new priorities are yet to come." This sentence works on the probability concept for that particular thing to occur. In some cases it does, and in some doesn't, not only for Gemini's but for other signs too.

In consequence, we will not be excluded from this cognitive error. Instead, we want to do it in a way that becomes healthier, not ignoring anything else by getting wrapped up in our ideas and concepts.

The following approaches can be used to minimise this effect. Use questioning skills, keeping an open mind, consider all the evidence available, challenge our own beliefs and opinions, embrace and tolerate new ideas. Beautiful and wonderful things can be found when we are exposed to what is different from what we already know.

VI
Perception vs actual experience

Considering the following classic example: Three persons are shown with a glass of water filled up halfway through. When the time comes for each person to describe how they see the glass - referring to its filled volume, person 1 sees it as halfway empty, person 2 as halfway full and the 3rd person believes the glass is too big for its purpose. There was no change in volume between the comments. Why are there 3 different views on the same thing? It comes down to our perception. The way we see, understand and interpret something. There is no right or wrong answer, it's simply based on the individual's perception in relation to that object. Each description has its own justification. It mainly derives from exposing factors such as emotional state, contextual background, personal traits and past experiences. Emotional state has the greatest influence on how we see something, whether optimistic, neutral or in doubt. Whenever a good feeling or a sense of optimism takes place, the way we see something changes. We are more subjected to interpret something as positive. Even if that's not the case in reality. As a result, we confront a form of disappointment – the difference between what we think and what we experience. The situation is not any different if the emotion is slightly gloomier. Our understanding of a situation can also shift, as we become more exposed to doubts and disbeliefs. Another important aspect of how a perception is interpreted relates to our own habits. Because we did it so many times before, we already pre-selected or pre-formed our opinions. If for the last hundred times, the way we saw the glass was half full or empty, there is no difference this time. Once we interpret something, it can become challenging to unsee it or see it in a different way. For example, consider two students facing an academic exam. One student finds an upcoming assessment as a stressful experience, while the other, an exciting challenge. Their contrasting emotional states drastically affect their perception.

Perception is attributed to various forms. Not necessarily as a physiological information in terms of touch, smell or hearing, but more like a combination between personality, thoughts, beliefs and ultimately the way we respond to specific scenarios. Perception can be defined as an inner reflection of how we see something at the time. Perception changes depending on the scenarios we experience and contextual information. For example, the 'overview effect' was described how astronauts' perceptions shifted immediately when they saw the Earth from space. Due do their intense emotions and profound experience, a collection of expressions was associated to an unthinkable and unimaginable moment. In other words, the captivating moment was a unique visualisation with an outstanding stimulus belonging to the world of fantasy. Back in 1987, some of them were interviewed to describe their experiences and their perception after travelling in space, more precisely on the Moon. The journey changed their perception of how they saw the life afterwards. To some of them, the experience had an enormous transformation in their lives. Charlie Duke became a 'transcendental meditator', only complying to voluntary work. Jim Irwin, later become a preacher. After the experience, they realised that the things they once considered important, no longer held the same value.

On a smaller scale of intensity, when travelling to different destinations and then returning to the original place, our perception changes even if the place itself hasn't changed. This can apply to both, more scenic destinations or less attractive ones.

After visiting a new place, on one hand, the original location may seem boring, while on the other-you might feel thankful for the place you currently live. In this context, people are often exposed either to gratitude or disappointment.

If we ask a dozen people to rate their perception of what they think about a specific job - we get various answers. Answers such us, "It's just a job", "It helps me to provide for the family", "It's quite stressful", "It's easy, boring", "It gives me the financial resource/motivation", "It's challenging", "I don't know anything else to do", "I love my job", "I have been doing it for 20 years." Perceptions vary from person to person depending on their personal experiences, genetic background and the way they see the world.

Perception is also shaped by our imagination before a situation occurs, rather than what happens during an event. On some occasions, a perception can be changed in no time and ultimately after. The reality, the living moment is based on the real experience, which is often different from our perception. This is due to an interaction with something or someone that can alter the result or response. For example, during a telephone conversation that goes out of hand. Before the event, you decided to be as reasonable as you can, calm and professional. As the conversation goes by, you become slightly impatient and concerned, leading you to raise the voice and possibly say something you should not have said. Therefore, the other person was less likely to help in the context given, leaving the initial request unresolved. Once the experience is ended, you began to realise that you should not have acted the way you did. Too late now. What could you have done better? We all find ourselves in similar situations at some point. Of course, we can use this experience to serve us as a valuable lesson to learn from and improve for next time. You couldn't know at the time, otherwise,

Perception vs actual experience

most likely you wouldn't have done so. Or perhaps there was some intention in it.

Perception	Reality	Perception
Before	*Actual*	*After*
What we think we should do	What we do	What we believe we should have done or do next time

Challenging our perceptions while holding a perception on the perception itself can be fundamentally important. Is it okay the way I interpret something? Is there another way to do so? Is it okay the way I think? What would I think if I wouldn't experience this? In some cases, some perceptions are only presented in our mind by what we choose to see and observe. Often, we may find these perceptions neutral or irrelevant. Can perceptions affect the decisions in our daily life? Certainly yes. They can direct our actions, intentions and choices. The way we look at something, often determines how we respond. However, during an event, feelings and thoughts can change, which alter perceptions and ultimately impact our decision-making process. Our behaviour often represents a by-product of those senses, we are more likely to act in a specific way - the way we 'show up' before an event. This highlights the need of a balance ratio between what we think and what we experience. In general, we should not forget that rationality plays its role when it comes to our perceptions and actions. Rationality, in this context, refers to the overall process – what happens before, during and after an event. It involves the property of our perceptions, thoughts and actions which are guided by a reason. Ultimately, on the basis to be more open to ideas and to tolerate what might be intolerable. To do that, we need to travel back to the 17th century, to learn more from the father of modern philosophy and rationalism,

Rene Descartes. The French philosopher and mathematician was well-known for the following sentence - *"I think therefore, I am."* His work was mainly emphasised on the methods of doubts, as most of his life he reflected on the false perceptions and premises he believed over the years. Moreover, he tried numerous times to doubt his own belief system and thoughts, whether they were true or not. By doing so, the sceptical process of doubting his own existence, proved to be true, otherwise he couldn't have done so if not alive. In this way the remarkable philosophical saying originated.

He often challenged his way of thinking to make his mind better equipped, prepared and to solve various significant problems at the time. His philosophical ideas were often characterised and distinguished by logic and reason, he argued that when trying to solve a difficult problem, it should be divided into one with smaller pieces but manageable. He also claimed the theory of ideas, which he considered as one of the most important aspects in his philosophy of thinking, representing a fundamental characteristic of the mind. Rene believed that the mind was superior to the body throughout thinking, ideas and analysing. The body, on the other hand was more subjected to mechanical laws. Moral reasoning was part of the mind. Morals that relatively serves as a foundation to human beliefs, obligations and the choices we encounter daily. (E.g., truth, justice - distinguish the difference between right and wrong, good and bad). With that in mind, perceptions contribute to a foundation of moral reasoning. What is morally right or wrong in a specific case? Is it okay to save an Amur leopard instead of a panda? You went shopping, the sales assistant missed to scan one of your shopping items, would you tell them? The difference between the mind and brain. The mind uses moral reasoning. It's more based on a virtual architecture, reasoning and judgment, while the brain, to a larger extent, engages in problem solving techniques and survival functions. Since we are probably challenged daily with it, moral reasoning represents a valuable characteristic considered one of the key elements for every human life and development; what we should do in a particular case, accept or not, what is morally good or bad.

We must not forget that logic and reason do not always lead to a good outcome. Especially, in a world where complex real-world nuances depend on the ability to allow flexibility and creativity when a situation demands so. As a result, individuals find themselves more likely to confirm their own existing beliefs without allowing a different perspective. Of course, that's not always the case otherwise all of us would be intellectually savvy, wealthy with good moral stories in the background, without resorting to unlawful acts. Things may not conform to a sequential order, particularly when something changes, or unfamiliar information takes place. For example, if I avoid risky decisions, the business I hold cannot go bankrupt. Or If I start saving for the next 5 years to buy a property, I will be able to get a home. There are many instances that logic and reason generally work. However, both cases do not guarantee a successful outcome. In the meantime, you may lose your job, encounter issues that delay your plans or other circumstances. This also applies when emotions influence our decisions, the choices that are not aligned with logical reasoning. The concept of logic and reason also depends on someone's abilities to form judgements based on environmental exposures that are encountered at the time.

4 couples attended 10 years anniversary dining. A cosy place is chosen as part of the service provided including a fine dining, live music in the background, a comfortable place and a good welcoming approach by the staff. At the end, they were all

asked for a review in terms of the service offered for the given price. The representatives of the venue wanted to get an insight if the prices are manageable to reflect the people's needs since it was newly inaugurated. As a note, they were all exposed to the same dining experience including a small variation between the selections. In addition, the food was prepared by a chef in front of the guests located on the 26th floor. After the experience, the first couple reveals: "It was a nice experience, just a little costlier than expected." The second couple mentioned that the price reflected the service they paid for. The third one enjoyed the time and considered it to be a bargain. The last couple was slightly disappointed with the service since they didn't have a large range of menu selections, the bill was way over the limit and the food didn't taste any better than at a conventional place. All couples had the same service provided. As a result, 4 different perceptions were brought up. These perceptions varied from couple to couple based on circumstantial factors such as, environmental exposure, personal traits, lifestyle and past experiences. However, if a large number of observations was used, most couples would fit into a single common review. This subject is further addressed in a different chapter.

As a result, perception shapes the way we look at something. It's established on individual beliefs, premises and experiences, rather than a group or the reality of others. What works for one doesn't for another. What holds significance or sparks optimism to someone might not be for someone else and the list continues. To develop a new perception or to alter the existing one, something needs to happen, a change in the environment, in the mindset or through different experiences. Perhaps, most importantly to acknowledge what we perceive. How can we change something it if we didn't know it needs a change? To rely only on the initial impulse of how something is captured at first instance, might not represent the right approach or even the contrary. In consequence, it's important to extend our perceptions. To be exposed to diverse life experiences, to various emotional states, to failure and success, to pain and gain, or volatile times. It gives us more ideas, thinking approaches, and solutions whenever we encounter different scenarios. We tend to realise that most of the things we think are important are no longer after or conversely, become more meaningful.

VII
A false sense of confidence

How good do you think you are in a particular subject in relation to your peers? Our ability to know how knowledgeable we are in relation to others is often more than a self-esteem improvement. It helps us to realise when to make progress on our conclusions and when we should instead seek alternative solutions.

Various psychological studies show that we are not so efficient at evaluating ourselves precisely. Moreover, we often overestimate our own abilities. This phenomenon is known as the Dunning-Kruger effect. The magnitude of this cognitive error was recognized in 1999 by psychologists David Dunning and Justin Kruger. In essence, this effect is used to indicate a false sense of confidence when someone has limited knowledge in a specific subject. The idea behind this concept indicates a misjudgement in our own abilities, which has an impact on our decision-making skills, giving poorer interaction in our workplace and society, and providing an inaccurate perception of how we see ourselves, the world and reality.

The Dunning and Kruger effect has been seen in various experimental studies that people show a false sense of superiority when it comes to rate their own competence levels. Individuals tend to judge themselves as better than their peers which sometimes breaches the law of maths. In one study, software engineers at 2 large corporations were asked to rate their own performance. At one company, 34% of the engineers rated themselves in the top 3%, while at the other this figure was

45%. In another analysis, it was found that around 80% of American drivers rated themselves better than the average, despite various statistics showing otherwise regarding the number of accidents involved. In addition, different studies were carried out emphasising on students to rate their performance after completing an exam in various disciplines such as inductive reasoning, literacy, and numerical tests. From the analysis, research has shown that the students who scored in the bottom 20th percentile overestimated their capabilities, ranking themselves above the 60th percentile even though the test scores suggested otherwise.

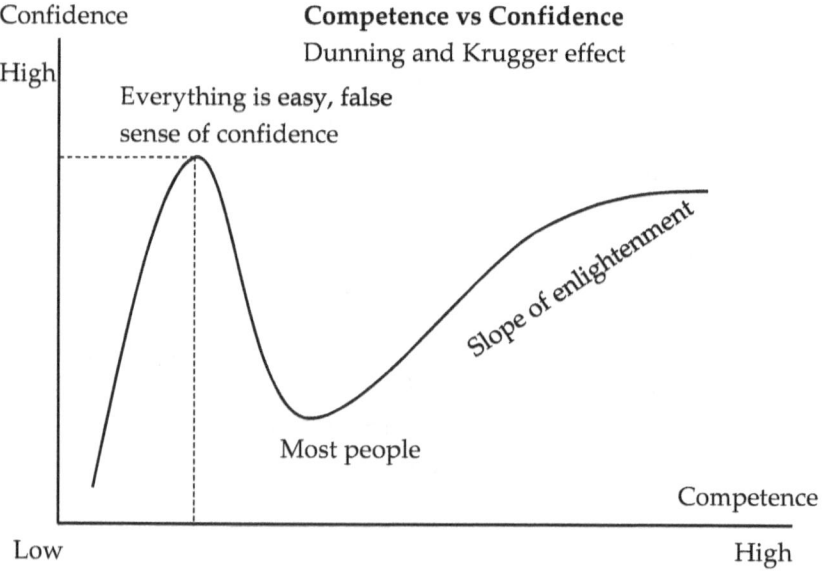

Often, people have the tendency to rate themselves better than the average. Interestingly enough, those with the least competence are frequently the most likely to exaggerate their performance. In other words, individuals with a lower competence in a particular area tend to have an overly positive perception. Research indicates that this is instead a false sense of confidence. With time, it gets converted into a more realistic one. Who is exposed to this illusion? All of us. Some people to a greater extent than others. This is largely due to the fragments of incompetence we don't even realise we have. This illusion is primarily focused on our metacognitive abilities. In other words, thinking about self-thinking. It's entirely based on the assumption that part of acquiring a skill consists in learning to distinguish whether the skill is the right or the wrong one, boosting or shrinking the confidence. Since people have not yet gained this skill, they cannot properly evaluate their competence. Thus, this will lead them to believe that they are better than they actually are when it comes to a specific domain. Competence is shaped by individual choices. Attributes such as attractiveness, time management, self-discipline, sympathy, kindness, effort-based performance, numerical ability are all part of one's specific subject of competence. Dunning and Kruger described this effect as a dual burden assumption. Firstly, people make errors and inadequate judgements and secondly the same errors stop them from noticing their faults. A good example of this phenomenon is described when someone passes their practical driving test on the 1st attempt. Normally, their perception of confidence rises more than it should. What if they were to have an accident during their practical test, they wouldn't believe so. In general, passing a test from 1 or more attempts doesn't necessarily mean that someone is competent in that subject. Graduates in the working environment who completed their first project or assignment efficiently, represent another exposure to this effect. Shortly afterwards, they tend to overestimate their own ability, mainly because they didn't develop the skill needed when a project is not delivered within the initial objectives. Alternatively, a different study shown, that graduates who had scored poorly on a numerical reasoning test and shortly after took additional lessons and training exercises, they considered their level of competence worse than the initial stage. People with a reasonable level of expertise tend to score themselves lower when it comes to their confidence level. "They are aware that there is a lot they don't know." Furthermore, specialists in a particular subject have the tendency to know about their own ability. Except, they make a separate misjudgement assuming that most people are just as experienced or sometimes inexperienced at all. As a result, from less knowledgeable to highly skilled, people are often falling victims to this effect. Individuals fail to recognise their own faults in relation to their own expertise or others'.

Whenever we face the Dunning-Kruger effect, of course if we know about it, what can be done to find out about our own abilities or how knowledgeable we are in a particular area? We can start with becoming more reasonable in our beliefs and conclusions, asking for feedback from time to time, keeping on learning, becoming aware of our own limits or knowledge, contemplating different viewpoints, and acknowledging we could also be wrong.

VIII
Human performance & effectiveness

Starting from 1890's onwards, different people have made certain affirmations along the way that we are only using 10% of our brain capacity. This assertion suggests that this percentage is the peak capacity during moments of high intelligence, while in normal times this number is significantly lower. It is believed that due to excessive information, if more than 10 percent would be used, it will create chaos within our bodily system, which eventually results in failure. The remaining 90% is therefore left as a spare size. However, this percentage of usage has not been proven scientifically. Even if one has access to the remaining brain capacity, it cannot be used due to its limitations needed for survival. It perhaps comes from its composition of 10% neurons, and 90% glial cells. Despite being studied for centuries, when involved in something complex, whether it's a novel or an innovation, it is still unknown what the brain's full potential is, and its undiscovered secrets. This number is primarily based on the assumptions from various medical institutions.

Why do some people learn easier and faster than others? At the age of 8, Bella Devyatkina, a Russian born citizen, was able to speak fluently seven different languages. German and Chinese were part of them. One of the reasons, she has probably been gifted with this talent of learning new languages, faster and easier than the rest of the world. Another possible reason is that repetition is often identified as the mother of all learning. In another instance, Magnus Carlsen, a Norwegian citizen, became one of the youngest world chess champions at the age of 21.

He therefore has captivated the world by showing a distinctive memory in the realm of chess, a sport often considered as a challenge for the mind that continually pushes new limits when it comes to abstract thinking and memory feats. Besides his professional achievements, Magnus is well known for his remarkable ability to play with 10 different opponents at the same time, without even looking at the table. He was able to memorise everyone's previous moves including his own, with all possible moves available and still able to win. Fascinating!

The human brain is often identified as the most complex system available, an interesting and distinctive phenomenon. With around 100 billion nerves cells and more than 100 trillion synapses, one of its aims is to analyse, subtract, extrapolate and add some of the functions designed for survival or conversely, to eliminate some of the ones which are no longer needed, mainly for the same purpose. Sometimes it is referred to as a muscle. The more it's used the better it becomes such as learning new things or becoming more adaptable when different scenarios may occur in the future. These events are kept in a gigantic storage like no other, called memories. History supports this information too. People were adapting to the environment, challenges, adapting to pain or gain, to different temperature conditions, social hierarchy, adapting to poverty or luxurious lifestyle, adapting to all kinds of scenarios offered by Mother Nature at the time. The mind uses anticipation almost for everything, travelling backwards and forwards in time, transforming any ideas or thoughts into tangible realities. It takes us to the most fascinating places, capable of extraordinary things, helps us to understand what happens around the world, enables us to learn new things, sends millions of signals to the other organs and creates some of the most fascinating marvels throughout history, such as *The Last Supper* or *The Great Egyptian Pyramids*. It also plays a significant part in our civilisation, working together and simultaneously as a team to share a common goal. Unfortunately, at the same time, it can also make people blinded, full of rage and influenced by power, leading to various tragedies, crimes and wars. It is within the individual to act appropriately according to their varying abilities. When a skill or talent is present, how can our commitments, decisions and actions give us the intended outcome that we really hope for? It doesn't happen instantly. It takes a long time until the best of the best is achieved.

The first internal combustion car

Automotive industry is chosen as an example of human performance, how it began, developed and maintained over time.

When attending any symphony orchestra event, you listen to the type of music which is created through the careful balance of many instruments by the craftsmanship of its conductor. Any unwanted noise, misbalance, or interruption would create an unpleasant sound to human hearing. Every violin, trumpet or any other instrument must be in balance and work simultaneously to release the desired sound. So too, the handling of a car, depends on the balance of many components and systems, grounded on engineering and physics, where every part plays its role to help the driver become the conductor of the car's symphony.

Have you ever wondered how a car works? How does it move? In simple terms, it translates the vertical motion from the engine through the crankshaft into a rotational movement to the wheels. You start the ignition, change gear, release the parking brake, and off you go. In some cars, the release of the parking brake might not even be required. In the meantime, everything happens simultaneously and in less than a second. The first phase starts in the combustion chamber, where a mixture of air fuel ratio is introduced to generate an initial pressure in the cylinder.

In the second stage, called compression, the same air-fuel mixture is compressed to be ignited. A set of valves are applied for opening and closing reasons in different cycles. The air-fuel mixture is then ignited, either through a spark plug or glow plug. The combustion phase causes the piston to move and initiates the crankshaft motion and subsequently creates the work required to propel the car. During the final phase of the exhaust stroke, a mixture of gases is released into the atmosphere, completing the four-stroke engine cycle. With the engine running, the idling condition does not move the car yet. When a gear is selected, for instance, automatic, the transmission unit uses planetary gears to rotate around a different gear called 'the sun gear'. A system of hydraulics, clutch packs and a torque convertor are integrated for changing gears at different rotational speeds. To transfer the power further from the engine through the transmission, a set of drive shafts, differentials and axles are used and interlinked to allow the necessary motion to the wheels. Due to the aim of this chapter, detailed and thorough description has been reduced.

In today's world of automotive industry, the cars offer comfort and provide high performance like never before including massaging seats, screening entertainment and luxurious artisanal devices. Some cars are more related to an art than a simple car, handcrafted to the finest details, reaching top speeds from 0 to 100km per hour in less than 3 seconds, featured by voice recognition commands or AI characteristics, and ultimately equipped with 5 stars safety features. Furthermore, when it comes to visual attraction, a car's silhouette is always aimed for aerodynamics and a design that has an inspirational purpose.

But it hasn't always been like that; the first practical gasoline engine was introduced in 1885 by Karl Friedrich Benz. He is identified and recognised as 'the father' of automobile industry.

The car was powered by an engine capacity of 954cc, generating less than 1 horsepower. Also, the automobile had a maximum speed of 16km per hour, single cylinder 4 stroke engine, supplied with steel-spoked wheels, solid rubbers tyres and a bench seat.

His revolutionary idea was to build the engine first and then the carriage around it. The car needed to have a mechanic on the passenger side due to the high probability of breaking down. Being not faster than a horse, the car faced substantial criticism from the public due to its lack of performance and limited range of less than 20km. They were also loud and noisy. Vehicle handling wasn't great either. Two years later, the unpredictable happened, when his wife Bertha Benz took the carriage and drove it up to her mother 120km away. The fast news spread in the society, sparked the attention of numerous people, becoming more and more interested to find out about the model. It was the trip that shaped the future in the car industry. Karl Benz then emphasised his attention fully on the model, exploring what improvements could be made.

In 1890, he introduced and patterned the planetary gear transmission, and the double pivot steering. In 1893, a more advanced and improved version was introduced, the Benz Victoria. Its engine output was 3 horsepower with a speed of 25km per hour. In 1894, Benz Velo was the first car in series production. It was a minor improvement over the first model created. In the meantime, the initial model attracted several people's attention, including different industrial designers and engineers.

**Benz Velo 1894, 1st series production car,
Mercedes Benz Archive Gallery**

Nearly a decade later, in 1901, Daimler Motoren Gesellschaft introduced the model, Mercedes. The engineering company was founded in 1890, by Gottlieb Daimler and Wilhelm Maybach. The car was able to reach up to 45mph with the engine power of 26kW. The model was named after a client's daughter's name 'Mercedes Jellinek'. Due to its high popularity and attention, the model then became trademarked in the company. As a result, Daimler chose to re-brand all their motor vehicles in that time to Mercedes. It was in 1926, when Benz and Daimler became partners, the Mercedes- Benz model came to life. By that time, numerous automakers made their mark in the automotive industry such as General Motors, Mazda, Alfa Romeo, Automobiles Lambert and many others. Due to the high demand in racing activities, Benz introduced in 1909, the 200-horsepower racer, named 'Blitzen Benz'. The model had a significant role on the company's future, which made the difference by breaking all-time speed records, reaching up to 225km/h. A few decades later, the introduction of speedometers, signalling,

Human performance & effectiveness

window regulators, mirrors and some additional safety features including the seatbelt protection followed. The Cadillac Sixty Special, launched in the 1940s by General Motors, featured the first automatic transmission. In 1951, the power steering control unit was available and included in a passenger car by Chrysler Corporation, aiming to reduce the effort needed for steering, particularly at low rotational speeds.

Up to the 1950s, motor vehicles were only affordable for the wealthy and rich, where the general population didn't have access to such luxury. Volkswagen's aim and purpose was to create one more affordable for the majority. The term 'Volkswagen' is derived from German, folks + wagon, meaning people's car. The company has done what they intended to with the model Beetle, also called 'Type 1'. The model experienced a continuous success, which was in production from 1938 to 2003.

From 1950's onwards, engineers from different automakers faced numerous challenges. One of them was to reduce the unwanted effects from an automobile when going over a harsh terrain, bump or uneven road. Part of the suspension system and to improve vehicle handling, the use of shock absorber was developed to reduce the concerned frequencies. Designed and patented by Bilstein, mono-tube shock absorbers were introduced in Mercedes cars in 1957. The company Ford, introduced in 1969, the antilock braking system, to improve vehicle manoeuvrability with the aim of a greater breaking efficiency by avoiding the wheels from locking up.

The basic principle of a car airbag was invented by John Hetrick in 1952, a discovery he considered by mistake. One evening, while he was driving with his wife and daughter through a cosy countryside, a baby deer pulled out from the forest in front of their car. In an attempt to avoid the collision, he and his wife moved their arms in front of their daughter to protect her. Its introduction into a mass production car was followed nearly 20 years later by General Motors in the model Chevrolet Impala. Electronic control unit called TLCS-12 was introduced by Ford in 1975. Just before the new millennium, various automakers introduced the adaptive cruise control. This was to maintain the vehicle speed without driver's input. To reduce the noise from the tyres, wind and other road unwanted sounds, Nissan introduced in 1992 the active noise cancellation to void any unwanted frequencies. In the same year, Audi introduced the aluminium monocoque design in its passenger cars with the A8 model. The aim for the light structure was, including safety, to create a lighter vehicle including a reduction in fuel consumption.

In the late '90s, the car performance was able to reach record speeds of 221mph, with an engine output up to 700 horsepower and 0-100km/h in 3.2 seconds, exemplified by McLaren F1. This record was not kept longer as Bugatti Veyron become the world's fastest passenger car in 2005, reaching an impressive top speed of 404 km/h with an engine output of 987 horsepower. Twelve years later, the company VW had the same challenge, but this time greater, to produce once more the world's most performing car. During this time, various automakers emphasised continuously on breaking the new record and advancing technology. Perhaps, the main aim appeared to be a pursuit of self-actualisation within the company requirements and to become one of a kind in the market. The incentive was to become faster, better than its competitors and eventually driven by the end user's wishes. With the new version of Chiron, VW's product development team adopted a new philosophy, to take the best from the previous model and improve it. Competition itself makes life easier to a slight extent, which facilitates access to different models and technology in the market. Bugatti Chiron was able to reach a new record in 2017, with a V16 quad-turbo engine and an output of 1479 horsepower, reaching from 0 to 100km/h in 2.3 seconds. Koenigsegg Agera reached a record speed limit of 445km/h. That's remarkable, compared to the first model output of less than 1 horsepower.

Nowadays, when we see a new car on the roads, its development began more than 5 years ago. Every year, different automakers encounter new challenges, pushing the limits of innovation by focusing on human-centred technology and continuously improving the product quality, safety, design and fuel economy. It doesn't just happen, it takes hundreds of thousands of hours through hardworking and careful planning, highly efficient personnel, to transition the concept development into realisation. Rigorous tests and simulations in between become a normal task in the daily routine, and ultimately it takes simultaneous engineering from all technical platforms across multiple disciplines before reaching the desired model that was planned years in advance. Also, everybody plays their part, from engineering to finance, development and marketing, manufacturing, logistics and other related functions. Advanced robotic systems and automatic guided vehicles, which are predominantly in use all the time, work 'hand in hand' with humans to achieve the ambitious goal of industry standard 4.0, an intelligent and flexible production.

The final touches are completed by a skilled and certified personnel who can see beyond the details before the final product is released on the road. With more than 30,000 components in a modern car, every part is tested and fully inspected before it's assembled into the next stage of production. This is to ensure the quality requirements and automotive standards are met. Functionality and aesthetics play their role too.

During vehicle testing and operation, it takes hundreds of thousands of tests kms in just a few weeks, an ageing process that completes a full lifecycle of a vehicle in just months, exposed to torrential rain, heavy snow, and extreme temperatures conditions tests. That's not all, it takes an aerodynamic design to withstand the natural forces of wind, in this case of more than 400 km/h to reach the anticipated record, and a vibration and harness test to understand the vehicle's behaviour for every gap and seam to the closest tolerances. And when it comes to painting, it takes feathers from the finest and biggest birds, to ensure flawless finishes. Timing, precision and coordination are more than just a daily routine to reach the desired outcome. This is where the people, parts, processes, and equipment are fully synchronised at the finest details to create the anticipated model. Ultimately, it takes innovative leadership to stand out from the crowd.

During the development stage, various process and phases are utilised to ensure that initial specification, functionality and requirements are met while reducing the project risks. One way to achieve this is through 'mock-up' samples. These samples are often increased in quantity for a more realistic interpretation as time goes by. They will first turn into prototypes to ensure the main functionality is met and after in real samples, just before the series production begins. In essence, the intended product goes through many processes along the development stage. Only through changes and testing in between the final product can reach its anticipated requirements.

If you want to dig deep in your pocket, Mercedes Maybach S680 might be an option, when it comes to exclusivity and ageless luxury. Beyond all, it takes 129 years of experience to see and reach such performance.

Human performance & effectiveness

2024 Mercedes Maybach S680, Mercedes Benz

To understand more what lies under this performance, something reoccurring is necessary to be reviewed and explored on a regular basis when it comes to human capabilities. The following pattern and process often lead to the anticipated result.

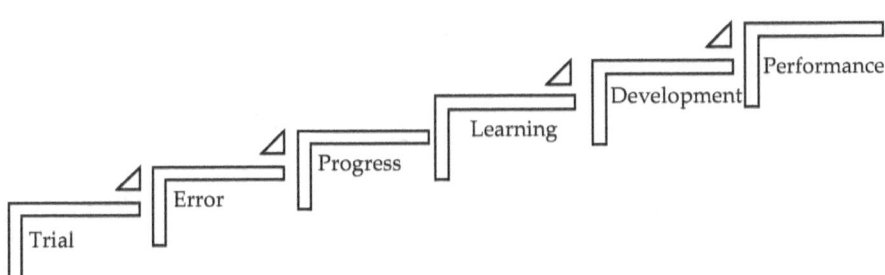

Firstly, during the trial phase, we may discover our unique and hidden potential or different possibilities that arise from it. Many wonderful things are discovered here. The penicillin, saving millions of lives every year, is one of them. Thomas Edison's light bulb discovery has been the platform of innovation in today's modern environment. Polymer, more specifically Polyacetylene, used in almost everything nowadays, represents another method discovered by a "fortuitous error". The groundbreaking discovery led to the Nobel Prize in the 2000's.

Often, people will have a greater chance of success and rate of performance if they embrace more trial opportunities. Most of the time, trial leads to errors or failures, which subsequently promotes progress, progress leads to learning, learning encourages development and eventually performance. In this context, errors are closely connected to failures. In the last phase, we can see the real contribution of the performance, taking the very best and improve it, but a series of phases is essential prior to reach such performance. The failure or error phase evokes many unpleasant feelings such as frustration, disappointment, and possibly a sense of abandonment. This depends on the individual or the group dynamic to confront such emotions and move forward to the next step. Each phase comes with different threats and opportunities. The failure phase gives the opportunity to approach things differently next time, the learning process probably becomes easier too. This is due to the emotional impact that is stored in our memories. One of the reasons is to avoid harm. Once we approach a certain stage, next time the way we explore similar situations changes significantly compared to our initial approach. After the first trial, if the outcome turns successful, an individual may experience the Dunning Kruger effect, which refers to a false sense of confidence. This perception will eventually evolve into a more realistic understanding of one's abilities. Between the learning and the development, lies the attention within a set of skills and how to use those effectively to make a real difference. Moreover, this stage involves the transition from the things that are learned to practical application. To step out from learning to development stage, it cannot be done only by acquiring a new set of skills but applying those in a real-world scenario that contribute to the desired change. Participating in various training programmes while still adhering to a gross conduct, 'nasty' with the people around, it becomes unlikely to foster development.

Secondly, challenging times make us more alert to change our behaviour to improve and to flourish. Different companies faced throughout history difficult periods from natural disasters, wars and deadly diseases. Some of them were able to bounce back in a timely manner. In other words, they developed resilience - a sustainable way to handling problems and unforeseen circumstances. During times of adversity, we are more likely to give our best potential. This is because it creates high alert frequencies to deal with the situation at the time. These challenging times create disturbances and high volatility between our emotions and behaviour, which can generate a better outcome with time.

Which person do you think is more likely to perform well? The one who is on a steady uplifting comfort zone or the one exposed to a greater volatility?

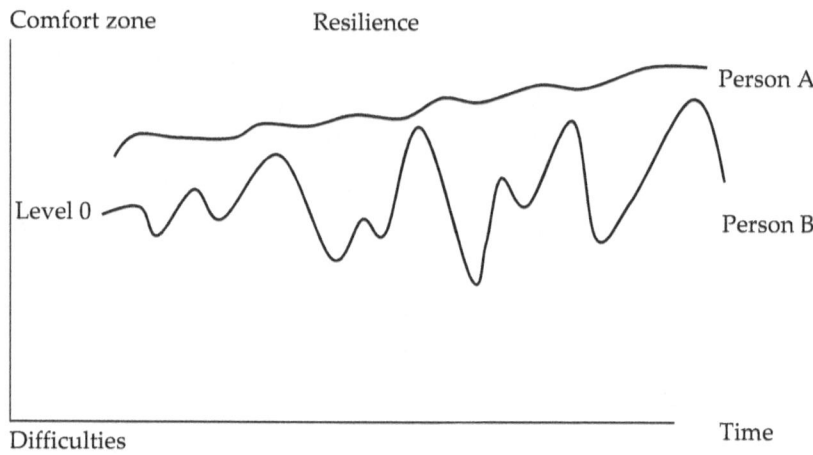

Any specific performance is not created and maintained with ease, comfort zone, and relaxation. However, these are obligatory and much needed between the phases as a recovery mode to go forward, start again, and prepare for the next challenges. What makes a company a great company? The people inside, diversity, quality of the product. If they are agile and perform well, there is a high probability that the company will too. In addition, the processes and tools that have been reviewed and improved for countless years in creating and sustaining the company's culture. When it comes to diversity, more identified in a cognitive way rather than an inclusion based on age, gender or ethnicity. This is because, solving complex problems cannot be done individually, but with high performance teams. This is due to the limited time allocated and high effort needed to solve such problems. Cognitive diversity refers to various thinking styles and approaches to solve problems. Knowledge, ideas, belief systems and personal experiences are considered too under this umbrella.

When cognitive diversity is present within a team, it broadens the number of solutions and ideas overall. By combining those, someone's weakness can transform the entire project in a good outcome. Cognitive diversity is designed to leverage the success of the project or its outcomes. In this case, it works as a puzzle where each person represents a unique form and shape that contributes to a common goal. If a group consists of individuals with similar backgrounds or viewpoints, they are likely to fall prey to confirmation bias, where certain ideas or content that need further exploration are frequently neglected. For example, each person comes with strengths and weaknesses. If someone acts quickly and swiftly in their decision-making process compared to a reflective person, they believe that the actions can be done easier and quicker just like them; in other words, underestimate the time required to complete a task. As a result, they tend to overlook some of the risks associated. On the other hand, a reflective person is inclined to take more time in the same process to evaluate different scenarios, which can lead to optimal results. However, they might struggle to initiate actions or overestimate the time needed to accomplish some of them. A team which embraces cognitive diversity increases the likelihood of success by generating more ideas as a group and achieving better results overall. A good example of this is the Bank of England, which employs someone completely outside of their expertise, to gain different perspectives and identify areas for improvement, to be more efficient in their decision process and projected time frames.

When looking closely at any specific performance, it's important to understand when we are more likely to be efficient, to give our best throughout the day. When involved in something complex or challenging, a psychological approach tool is described by Robert Yerkes and John Dodson in 1921 on how the human performance is correlated during this stimulus.

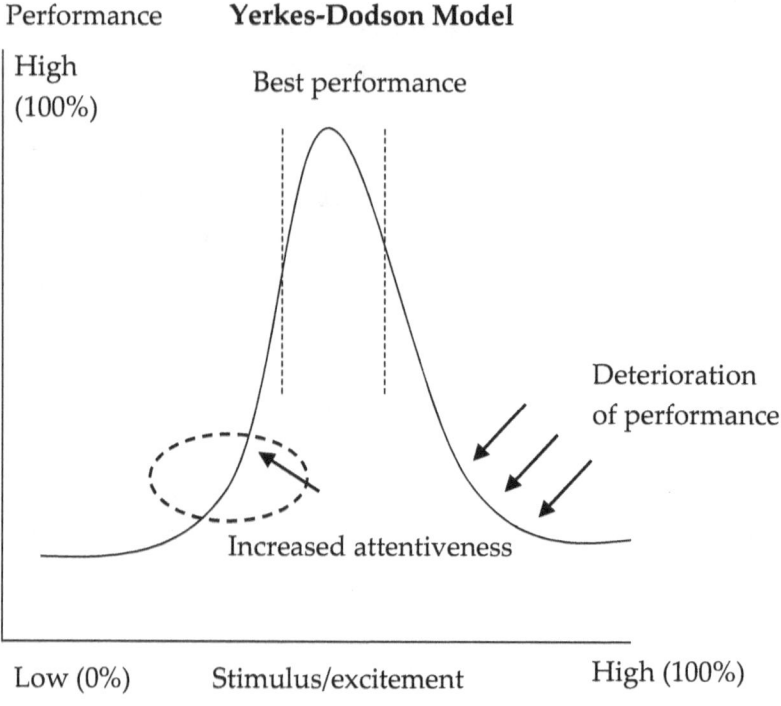

Mostly, the performance increases only to a certain degree depending on the situation at hand. Stimulus, in this case, refers to factors such as motivation, excitement, level of tension or conflict. Normally, we tend to give our highest efficiency when we face challenges relative to our own abilities. However, if the level of challenge intensifies or declines, our performance will be reduced. For example, if your own ability in a particular subject is 70%, an extra 5-10% could generate a good result. In opposition, when the level of pressure is much higher than we can cope, it becomes overwhelming, thus the performance declines.

Whenever various challenges are present, it's important to recognise how we should approach them. Every day we are subjected to, it comes with neural oscillations. More specifically, the brainwaves or the electrical signals in our nervous system that display recurring patterns and responses throughout the day. There are 5 brainwaves that we encounter every single day:

Neural Wave	Description
	Alpha (8-12Hz). Calmness, restfulness, abstract thinking, passive attention
	Beta (12-28Hz). Active, dynamic, alertness, fear, worries, disturbance
	Delta (0-4Hz). Sleeping, restoration, indolence, inactivity
	Theta (4-8Hz). Relaxation, drowsiness, intuition, laziness, fatigue, boredom, tiredness, sadness, auto-pilot mode
	Gamma (28-35+Hz). Concentration, high active attention, problem solving, stress

These waves are displayed frequencies, active throughout the day and night, ranging from 0.1 to 35+ Hz. It's never 0, not even we are at sleep. From low to high intensity, they continuously change depending on the present moment, which create different effects on our bodily system. Frequency is measured in Hertz, the number of wave cycles per second. Every wave is important and has its role, keeping the balance greatly needed.

The delta phase, also called the recovery wave, has the lowest frequency range with the highest amplitude. The amplitude refers to the height of variability. Amplitude represents the voltage measured in microvolts. For the purpose of this chapter, the amplitude's measurement is not represented on the graph. A typical person's amplitude, ranges from 10 to 100 microvolts. In the beta phase, both states can be found, in the same line of intensity but on a different spectrum, positive and negative. For example, alertness and increased energy level or disturbance and agitation. Similarly for other waves. This wave is associated when we are active and consciously prepared for engagement in various activities. Theta wave is where we are most likely to display most of our emotions and engage in slower activities such as relaxation, mind wandering, daydreaming, halfway sleeping, tiredness or the absence of energy. Gamma is primarily related to a high frequency range, from problem solving, to high alertness with the ability to learn and perform. It gives the person the fastest stimulus response. However, this wave can also lead to the other side of the spectrum such as worries, panic and stress.

The first three phases (delta, theta, alpha) display lower levels of activity, while beta and gamma are associated with higher levels. During which time of the day are we most likely to experience these brain waves? Let's take a closer look at how these electrical signals are shown and when they are more likely to occur. In a normal working day, following a good night's sleep, an individual may experience the following sequence:

Feeling calm and relaxed soon after waking up, probably on autopilot or involved in the morning routine. Not long after, engaging into beta wave, ready to act and participate in various activities. Soon, if exposed to gamma phase, the person is more likely to perform well. This is when we are most likely to give our highest efficiency for the day. Highly motivated, ready to tackle any issues or challenges with an ability to learn faster and easier. In other words, a high focus towards solving problems. During this time, it's necessary to concentrate on the most important tasks of the day. A little while later, this wave tends to dissipate, probably we experience sensation of hunger, and slight tiredness varying from lower to higher intensity depending on the individual. As the person waits for lunch, to regain energy and enter the restore function, they might slip in the low alpha zone or high delta, hopefully not falling to sleep or daydreaming. If the environment allows you, it's probably not a bad thing. That's because if doing so for a short time, soon after waking up, the recovery process is easier, meaning that we are more likely to engage in the beta or gamma phase faster than normal, which helps in the problem-solving approach.

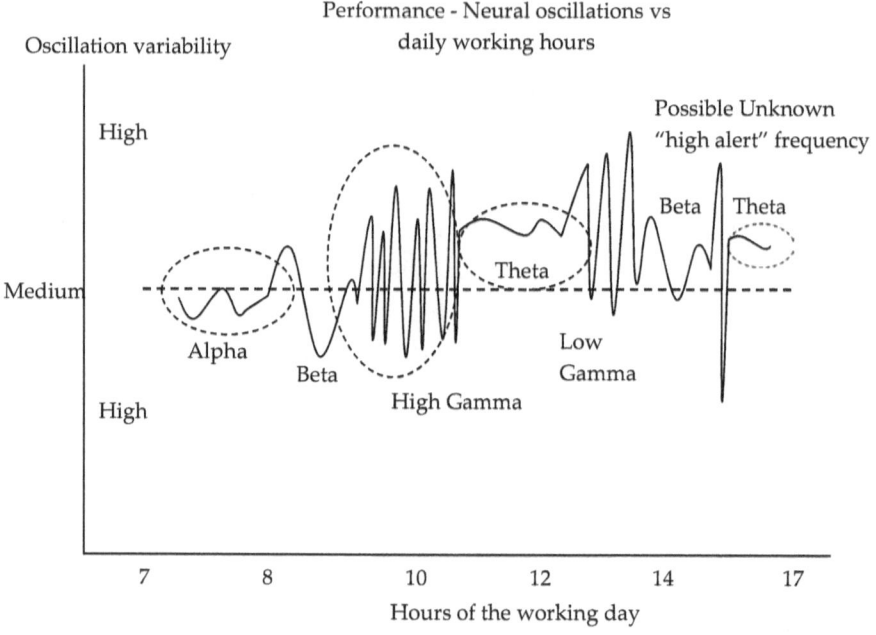

Different studies have shown that taking less than half an hour of sleep during the day can improve performance, productivity, and reaction time by 20%. However, exceeding this time, can have the opposite effect, making the situation worse, shifting from theta to delta, making harder to perform well. The next few hours, the person alternates between alpha and beta, and probably in lower gamma if the situation requires to do so. If a task requires a substantial amount of time before the working schedule ends, the person may disengage from completing it. As a result, they might enter a 'waiting time zone' to leave the premises, already disconnected from any activities and perhaps in the theta wave. In other words, "Having done enough for the day!" There are several factors that influence such order including the work environment, job requirements, individual's routine, and personal traits. Occasionally, we are exposed to high-frequency alerts throughout the day. Usually, these frequencies are unknown and unpredictable, which can derive from various sources or news, good or bad. Life itself presents us with scenarios that expose us to such unknown frequencies from time to time.

According to research, out of 8 working hours, we are only productive for approximately 4 hours. The rest of time is spent on different activities or non-value-added ones such as attending meetings, phone inquiries, checking social media, smoking, regular breaks or unrelated communication. Furthermore, Stanford University's research indicates that working more than 50 hours a week, an individual's performance starts to decline when compared to the weekly average of 40 hours or less. The performance of an individual can be linked to different electrical waves depending on the subject, where creativity and calmness can often make a real difference, but gamma wave, in general, provides the most likely frequency to achieve our potential.

From slow to fast activity, these brainwaves serve us with a momentum, protecting us as we go along, offering the balance and harmony needed every day. The restoration wave, experienced between days, has helped countless individuals to solve problems or challenges that they couldn't on the previous day. Feeling better, providing new perspectives, and using different problem-solving techniques are all covered within this recovery mode. These brain waves offer numerous hidden activities to look after us and help us to function effectively depending on the situation at hand. In essence, it's important to recognise the pattern of these oscillations and the likelihood of those to happen in relation to the individual's routine. There is only one reason, to work hand in hand with those waves for something to be done more efficiently in a given context.

"A fascinating story" ... nothing more, nothing less

In the early years of the new millennium, the Clay Mathematics Institute published a list of seven unsolved problems in the field of mathematics. Those problems have been considered the most difficult in the world, which are identified as significant 'representations' of the reality we live in. For this reason, the institute assigned a prize of 1 million dollars as a reward for each problem solved. Grigori Perelman fascinated the world with his contributions in the subject of differential geometry and analysis. In 2002, he solved one of them, known as the 'Poincaré Conjecture', in the field of topology. Grigori Perelman was born in 1966 in St Petersburg, Russia. Since early childhood, he developed a strong inclination for mathematics, as he was challenged by his parents to solve different puzzle games. By the age of 16, he had developed an exceptional talent, wining several math competitions in geometry, inspiring one of the professors with his ability to think 'beyond' the scenes. In 1990, Perelman finished his Ph.D. in Euclidean geometry research. Solving one of the most challenging problems in 2002, he remains as one of the greatest living mathematicians. The seven problems are considered extremely difficult to solve due their complexity and magnitude, where some people may spend a considerable amount of time even decades trying to solve one of them without reaching a feasible conclusion. As a result of his achievement, Perelman was awarded a prize of one million dollars and the Fields Medal in 2006, an honour considered the equivalent of a Nobel Prize in mathematics. Despite his remarkable insights and knowledge, the reason why this is a fascinating story, he refused both, the prize and the award medal. Even more surprising is that during that time, he was living with his mother, while his financial situation might not have been not the 'greatest'.

Grigori Perelman surprised everyone at the institute with his decision, stating: *"I'm not interested in money or fame; it was irrelevant to me; I don't want to be on display like an animal in a zoo."* His approach showed the world that, in the face of a mathematical challenge, achieving recognition is not what truly matters, even when he has accomplished something entirely based on his own merits. Just take a moment to imagine how difficult this must be to refrain from such a prize. Giving something away comparatively to a much smaller offer of few digits - with or without merit - can be quite challenging. Grigori Perelman displays a distinctive contrast to greed, arrogance, and selfishness, exemplified by humility, modesty, and selflessness to the finest details. He created history for his remarkable performance and narrative behaviour.

IX
Fundamental attribution error

When you drive on a busy highway, and someone suddenly pulls in front of you or drives too slow, one of the many profanities crossing your mind is, "What an absolute idiot!" and that's a gentle way. One of countless examples available. Interestingly, when this is done by yourself it's not that bad. It's a coincidence or you try to find the most explanatory reason for it. You might say, "Hey, relax, I had no other choice, I'm tired, or I have an emergency." Why engage in this phenomenon without considering all the potential facts? They probably had a reason for it too, it could have been a medical emergency or attending a funeral. If you see someone lying in bed watching TV, you might think they are lazy. When you do it, you have been working hard and now relaxing. The tendency of assigning judgmental characteristics to someone's character without considering the limitations or constraints, but when it comes to their own, often denying the error or fault, considering it was a circumstantial factor. This is known as the fundamental attribution error. The term 'fundamental' comes from the high usage of what we see and experience in the environment.

What would you say if someone you love (excepting your partner) committed an immoral act, more specifically if they engaged in adultery? Suppose their actions were motivated by unspecified reasons. Would you be supportive and take their side? Take a moment to think about it...! Now, what would you think if the same act was done by someone unknown to you?

In recent years, some of these examples of attribution errors appear more and more common in our daily lives and throughout society. What lies under this cognitive error? Initially, we tend to explain our own behaviour more accurately as we have more information about what happens at the time. In contrast, when we attribute someone's actions, we have limited information or insufficient details about what the other person experiences. Additionally, this phenomenon occurs when we sense a lack of control over a situation. When we have no control in a certain case, it's easier for us to make judgements that protect our self-esteem. In this case, it works as a self-protection mechanism, preventing an internal or external conflict to escalate, sometimes even enhancing our self-esteem. The question is, "Is it the real self-esteem?" On the other hand, this often leads to frustration and a false sense of self-perception. Therefore, we don't want to interrupt the pattern of our own belief systems, especially when doing so that makes us feel at fault or uncomfortable. When we engage in attribution error, we 'think' it is easier for us to accept the situation as it is, not as we wanted it to be. The human brain is dealing constantly with many situations at the time - conflicts, challenges, problems, information and so on. When a decision must be made, the aim is to neglect and ignore some of this information and instead seeking 'shortcuts'. If a shortcut is presented as an opportunity, then the brain will decode and transfer it immediately, engaging the individual in so-called behaviour. After all, this tendency comes from the practices that people often participated in previously. If an uncomfortable event makes us accountable in some cases, it is largely due to how something is perceived at that time. Another contributing factor to this error is illusionary superiority, where some people may overestimate their own abilities. An approach in their belief system, thinking they are greater, smarter or more attractive than their peers. A large number of people have the tendency to be confident and occasionally too confident in their own beliefs and judgements. In other words, they put themselves in a higher hierarchy, although the findings would suggest otherwise, especially when compared with the average people. A study conducted among students at a Business Management School revealed that more than 85% rated themselves as better than the average. A similar analysis from Harvard University, with more than 5000 participants, showed that most people believed they would meet a specific set of criteria established at the beginning of the study. Only less than 15% fitted in the requirements proposed, regarding their own qualities. Delusion of grandeur is another ingredient that lies under this cognitive blunder. A person assigns a greater importance to their belief systems, imagining that they are special, have extra powers or magical skills, when this is often not the case. This irrational confidence can sometimes 'blind' individuals or make them too proud, leading to distorted perceptions and opinions when it comes to their own judgements. When paying a closer attention to what surrounds us, we may be able to see the sky, the clouds, the flora in its best natural form and shape. If darkness is present, the stars and moon are envisioned. We might develop a different perception afterwards. We tend to realise the observation we've had initially is not that important as we thought it was.

If someone is late for a meeting or work schedule, you might say, "This person is a bit sloppy, they waste my time or are not punctual enough." At the time, it may seem a valid point, especially if it happens once or from time to time. When you do it, you are trying to find x number of reasons why you are late, which contributes to a change in your response. "I was held up in a different meeting" or "There is a long way from my office to get here". When someone is caught in an act of dishonesty or not following specific norms, we might be exposed to phrases like: "This is such an irresponsible behaviour!" Besides our personal beliefs, this reaction may correspond further within our ethical or working environment norms. In contrast, when it comes to our own conduct, different scenarios are brought up: "I had no other way", turning the page upside down, "You don't know all the details", or "I would have never done something like that!" This can happen both consciously and subconsciously.

The fundamental error can be extended into 2 other categories:

- *Self-serving scenarios.* This is observed when someone attributes a favourable outcome or success solely due to their own personal skills or qualities, while in the case of a negative outcome, they often suggest that there was a circumstantial error, bad luck or other people's fault. E.g. If you work on a project, and achieve a positive result, you only give yourself credit. If the project is not as you expected, the attention is shifted somewhere else rather than your own contribution such as other people's involvement or time limitations. "We won because we trained harder, we played better"; in case of losing – "We were disadvantaged by the weather conditions or referee". Another example is when an individual brings a point of discussion only when it's favourable to them.
- *The actor-observer approach.* This error occurs in a situation where an individual as an actor, would find the error in the external factors. Alternatively, as an observer watching someone else, would ignore any external factors and would find the other person at fault as an internal trait. For instance, if someone has a low performance you think they didn't prepare enough or were careless, when you do it, you were tired due to a busy schedule and lack of sleep.

These ethical blunders are manifested further in a way that we expect someone to have a certain characteristic or conduct, but we often fail to observe our own. Unable to remember our own hitches and glitches. Often, this attribution error can lead to hypocrisy. We expect someone to follow a certain action or conduct, but we don't do it ourselves. Someone asks us to help the environment, but themselves drive fast cars. We expect someone within a project team to work long hours, and we are the first ones to exit the premises. We desire a clean and tidy place, and we are the first ones leaving the unwashed dishes in the sink. We expect someone to be more compassionate and understanding, but what are we offering instead? We expect someone to be honest and transparent, and when we look deeper within ourselves, we find out there might be room for improvement.

Under some circumstances, there are exceptions when there is no pattern or explanation in these ethical blunders. While I was on my way to a shop in the city centre trying to find a parking space, I noticed someone who had left their car unattended in front of three other cars, blocking them from exiting. That was interesting since there were numerous parking spaces available in the close vicinity. I couldn't find a real explanation; it seemed almost intentional.

What would you like to see more of in this world? One way to make a good impact when it comes to the environment we live in, whenever we want to see a change, perhaps we should start with ourselves first. Not to disagree or expect what someone else should or shouldn't do. We know from research that our conduct or actions can be transmittable. The way something is manifested by us, it increases the likelihood for another person to be exposed more to the same conduct in the future. For instance, if you expect someone to be more transparent and honest, you should start with yourself first by doing so. One common approach to avoid assigning these fundamental errors is to acknowledge what you experience at the time. Additionally, it might be beneficial to challenge our assumptions and how these are represented when it comes to our own circumstances and actions. Fallibility could be another valuable approach to overcome this error of judgment.

X
Perfect fairness, the irrational expectation

"When 2 monkeys were paid unequally"

Franciscus Bernardus de Waal, professor at Emory University, spent his entire academic life specialising in ethology. His research in primates and eventually in relation to human behaviour, attracted millions of viewers around the world. Inequity aversion was one of the topics within his area of expertise when he carried out an experiment between 2 monkeys. More precisely, Capuchin monkeys. For this narrative, they are named monkey Alpha and Betha.

The outline of the experiment:

Both Capuchin monkeys were taken from the same group of their co-habitat and afterwards placed in separate cages close to each other. As part of a task, they both were required to give a small stone in exchange for a slice of cucumber as a reward. They did that several times while they were both satisfied with the reward given. Since one of the Capuchin's favourite foods was grapes, monkey Betha receives grapes as a reward instead of cucumber. Shortly after, monkey Alpha gets the same food, a slice of cucumber in return for the stone. This unfair treatment caused monkey Alpha to become agitated and distressed, rejecting the slice of cucumber and threw it at the researcher's assistant. Before the introduction of grapes, they were both content with the similar food given as a recompense. This became unacceptable for monkey Alpha to see and witness a different prize provided for similar efforts. Monkey Alpha refused to eat the slice of cucumber simply because monkey Betha got a better reward.

Furthermore, this is extended in human behaviour, where the deterrent key of unfairness between two or more individuals is strongly influenced by social comparison. Various occasions and evidence suggest that the desire for fairness is often hidden, even among the brightest of us.

What lies under the principles of fairness moral and how important is it?

To begin with, the feelings of having a natural desire for fairness as an individual or within a group, is completely normal, embodied in all of us. From time to time, this feeling becomes even stronger as we crave for fairness in almost everything we do. Renowned as the happiest country in the world, Finland experiences fairness within its community that contributes to their overall happiness. When this sense of fairness is threatened, it creates discomfort, frustration, and feeling of inequality within society. In other words, when fairness applies to us, it creates a good outcome that works for everyone involved. For example, consider two individuals who have worked at the same company for 5 years. They are both approximately the same age, possess similar professional and academic experience. They hold the same title and role too. If one of them earns, for instance 20% more than the other, this difference will likely evoke the same feelings of unfairness and ethical concerns.

The perception of fairness or unfairness largely depends on the outcomes one receives in response to their efforts, whether those outcomes are favourable or unfavourable. For example, "If someone treats me nicely, I will treat them nicely too." The opposite applies too, addressed resentfully. This follows the well-known expression, "An eye for an eye and a gift for a gift." However, strictly adhering to this principle may not work effectively in the society we live in, where everyone may end up metaphorically blind. Opinions and behaviours are spread differently when it comes to this expression, where many individuals disrupt this cycle by not responding in the same manner, particularly not in a revengeful act.

Fairness is often addressed when individuals make judgments from their point of view of what is right or wrong. If any impartial treatment is 'seen' or forecasted, it can lead to unpleasant states such as annoyance, disappointment, and resentment. These feelings often stem from our expectations and perceptions, where we create an imaginary concept that we will get rewarded when an effort is made. E.g. If I invest the necessary hours and effort in project 'y', I will get rewarded accordingly. Probably, most likely, but not certainly. Not every effort will yield success, resulting in a good outcome or adequate recognition. In a startup business, the likelihood of success is approximately 20% in the first year of trade. Furthermore, only 30% of the new businesses show an average result within the first 3 years. Let's say, 95% of business owners want their ventures to succeed, (not 100% due to unspecified reasons). They do whatever it takes from planning, preparing, working long hours, based on their business needs and associated risks. With the best intentions, probably every single one of us desires a good outcome when it comes to a startup business or anything of the kind, but doesn't necessarily mean that we will get rewarded accordingly.

Furthermore, fairness is defined when we expect that everybody else holds this moral as a stone in their background to conform in the same way as we want. Simply, an imaginary concept we all encounter. This concept approach is called Kantian Fairness. It originates back to the 18th century, from the father of morals and ethics, Immanuel Kant (1724–1804). Kantian fairness along with many others such as respect and beneficence, are a set of morals that apply to all humankind. These ethics are also known as the Kantian ethics. Immanuel Kant spent his last 2 decades writing and publishing the 'Metaphysics of Morals', which focuses entirely on ethical virtues and the philosophy of morals.

The implication of morals in daily life was a question of taste, opinion, and sentiment. People's views were varied from one person to another. Someone favoured different food, music, colour or even a belief system to distinguish between the good and the bad. On these grounds, Immanuel Kant thought that morals are just an illusion or a false belief. This notion bothered him enormously. He proposed that moral decisions should be spread equally, to all human beings. The German philosopher then divided those judgements in two types: *perfect and imperfect duties*. A perfect duty requires a moral obligation either to oneself or to others. For example - keeping a promise, a mutual agreement, telling the truth, protecting own life. In contrast, an imperfect duty allows flexibility and cannot be measured with accuracy. This implies when a person chooses to do so but they are not morally responsible for it, helping someone in need, being kind or compassionate. He claimed that *fairness* is a *perfect* duty, which embraces accurate information at all times. According to Kant's work, there is only one type of moral principle that always qualifies for the truth, categorical imperative. Immanuel Kant describes this moral as a universal law, which everyone must follow. In other words, it represents a duty to ourselves to act in a way that we expect anyone else to act towards other people. Therefore, Kantian fairness lies under the categorical imperative framework.

When an individual is highly dependent on the principle of 'perfect fairness', it can cause disappointment and discomfort, partly because this expectation has been ingrained in most of us since early stage. There are a few ways how a person can deal with unfairness when they experience it:

- The admiration perspective. At some point in our lives, during our teenagers years or lately, we have probably been asked before: "Who do you admire the most and why?" In this context, there is a person in our mind that we wish to be like, because it lines up with our values and aspirations, thinking about the attributes and qualities that the person may offer at the time, and we don't, yet.

- The nature of jealousy. This arises when an individual desires traits or possessions that someone else has. Common examples can derive from moral dimensions, financial assets, beauty and more. This feeling comes from social comparison with or without intention. Ignoring the unpleasant consequences what the jealousy may offer with this occasion, it isn't necessarily harmful - but instead beneficial - motivating individuals to become closer to the other person, showing a self-improvement approach to achieve their goals or perhaps to be in trend with the society we live in. Jealousy is also found on the basis when someone feels threatened by the potential loss of 'something' that is important to them. Sometimes, we are exposed to such scenarios, because we fail to remember our own morals and values, what is important to us and not to others.

- The envy. This state applies when one of the contributing factors derives from an unfair advantage and social comparison. We know what happened in the case of monkeys! One instance of many others amongst the general population. Considering this, there will always be someone who appears to be prettier, smarter, thinner, wealthier and so on – unless that someone really is. It can be extremely upsetting if "your friend is getting rich while you get stuck in a 9-5 job". Moreover, the word 'rich' has a broader context not just on a financial basis. Someone can be rich in their heart, knowledge, or character. With that in mind, it's important to ask yourself: How important is that to me? Most of the times you tend to realise it isn't.

Gerald and James knew each other as neighbours for some time. They both prioritise their families while, in general, enjoying a comfortable lifestyle. When it comes to financial metrics, they both are on good terms too. They work as investment bankers for a prominent institution within the local area. James has 6 digits figure income, while Gerald earns slightly less - about 5% less, to be exact. Not a lot, considering the large scale at which they operate. Sometimes, they meet over lunch to catch up with the news. One of the topics brought up is the annual earnings, which is typically considered a confidential matter. Gerald feels a twinge of irritation when he finds out about James's earnings. He finds himself questioning in his mind how James earns more than him, despite sharing a similar background and level of experience. Gerald only pays attention to the small percentage of why the other person is better off, instead of concentrating on his own high earnings and family, enjoying the most he can. Due to the perfect fairness that Gerald is subjected to, he is dealing with disappointment and irritation instead. His entire focus on the small percentage of incentives makes him to overlook the larger scale of his own success.

Expecting perfect fairness can often evoke many unpleasant feelings such as resentment and unhappiness. This is because an individual measures everything on a scale of fairness while they do not accept or tolerate any impartial treatment even to the smallest tolerance. In a romantic relationship, there are no exceptions to this tendency. Expecting total fairness from your partner. Imagine you have a day off and spend it tackling the household chores and preparing dinner, not only for your partner, but for you too. For some reason, the tasks were only partially finished. Next day, your partner has a day off. They mentioned they feel tired and exhausted from work and plan to use the day to relax, with no commitments and engagement in any activities. Meanwhile, you have long day at work, but you believe it's only 'fair' that your partner to finish the remaining tasks or at least prepare dinner since they had a day off.

There have been similar scenarios recently. Now, because of the most vivid experience, you feel that lately, you offer something more than the other person. But in this case, it's only fair as your partner affirmed their needs and plan to use the day as recovery mode, so they can enjoy the evening together, rather than being neglectful or itchy. Because of this, one partner feels irritated, as they expected everything on the ideal scale of fairness. The situation gets worse over time, as the irritation intensifies leading to a growing distance between them, while the flowing love starts to diminish.

As an individual, to demand a strict balance of 50-50% fairness can lead to various consequences and far from positive ones. Once we start to keep a score, it often evokes many hidden feelings and hitches. To expect perfect fairness is neither functional nor realistic. Life is unfair to some people or more favourable to others, regardless of their effort applied. Acknowledging this concept, tolerating that not everything is fair, can helps us manage these scenarios more effectively. Above all, it's essential to avoid expecting such ideal fairness from the beginning.

XI
Vivid and unreliable memories

William, 38 years old, is a senior project manager at a large corporation that specialises in quantitative finance. He has been with the same company for over a decade, progressing steadily up the corporate ladder. Throughout his tenure, he has participated in 23 projects, guiding them from start to finish over the years. He successfully completed all the projects within their objectives set from the beginning, including timeline, and budget constraints. William was an employee model for many years. He had also no absences or real complaints from any party. Recently, he is assigned to a completely new project. William is given the role to lead the project, since he was the most appropriate and skilful person at that time. The scale and importance of the project are within the same ordinary effects from the past. William is extremely determined and excited about the possibilities that this scenario presents. When the timeline is near, William couldn't finish all the initial objectives, and the cost calculations were also exceeding the limit. William entirely admits that the project was slightly slippery, and he takes full accountability for it. He completes a lessons learned document with what went wrong and right, to avoid the same mistakes in the future. William also states that another reason was due to a family problem related recently (in the time being resolved), and his insights and focus were not at the highest level, and next time he will be more cautious.

The project was a novel within the company history and not been tested before. Therefore, it was a challenge for the company as well as for William. In addition, the project had different turns or unforeseen circumstances that caused the slight delay. Not long after, a different project is assigned approximately of the same level of significance. Now, the board management states that William's competence wasn't the highest in contrast to his past performance, and therefore considers he is not the appropriate person to lead the project this time.

What could William have done better? What about the management?

Because of the most recent project William was involved in, the board management only recalls what went wrong. Additionally, the most vivid experience caused the management to believe that the previous project was more important in comparison to the last 23. Therefore, this led to a conclusion that the recent project became more memorable especially when the decision was made. The management did not consider any previous data as a guide or looked at the overall picture. Their conclusion was based purely on the most recent activity, ignoring any relevant information from the past. William also didn't know how to react in some circumstances, and therefore the project was delayed to some extent, partially because it was one of a kind project. Could he have known all the possible scenarios or turns related to the project? Most likely not! He has done the best he could at the time. Or perhaps he should have communicated more effectively beforehand to the relevant team, to avoid the delays. We don't want to fall victims as William when it comes to our own judgment to make better choices and decisions. One reason behind this approach is because the management acted only according to the most recent and vivid experience rather than observing the event based on the whole picture. Ignoring or rejecting any relevant information from the previous history.

This is just an example amongst many others, where our most recent experiences seem more important from the past. In an ever-changing world, we tend to make quick assumptions and conclusions when a decision must be made. Another key reason is that approaches that worked well in the past create a desire to replicate those successful outcomes. While this can appear efficient, we don't want to become overwhelmed by weighing every possible scenario from previous events. On the other hand, it distorts our perspective, leading to faulty reasoning and misleading conclusions. Other significant factors contributing to these 'false' memories may be related due to the time constraints and the pressure to conform, particularly when a decision must be made quickly. Additionally, in environments where critical decisions are made continuously (surgery, air traffic control, engineering, etc), decisions can be made due to incomplete information. Sometimes, the choices that are made can save lives, while at other times, they may cloud our judgment and prevent us from effectively interpreting what happens at the time. The ability to make quick decisions often depends on specific circumstances, as we frequently have limited time to evaluate every possible scenario from the past. It is the brain way of coming up with fast responses and decisions.

In a romantic relationship, this happens more frequently. For example during a point of debate, conflict or argument where someone draws a conclusion too soon based on the most vivid experience. I believe, an 'argument' is needed from time to time in any relationship as long as it's productive. At the end, it is not so much about the argument itself, but the way how it is repaired. Arguments are brought up due to numerous causes grounded on influence, caring, financial topics or unfairness. Maria and John are seeing each other for some time. They both consider themselves to be a happy couple, doing activities together, sharing the life's experience, with the same beliefs but with some differences too. Six months into the relationship, they both like each other's companionship and are trying to move the relationship to the next step - moving in together. They have been living together for several years now, 5 years to be exact. As a result, they decided to get married the following year. During this time, as probably any other conventional couple, they had some arguments over the years. Some of them more intense than others. On this occasion it was nothing out of the ordinary. Maria didn't like when John left the wardrobes open. Marie informed John about her wish right from the start. Her wish was solely based to avoid dust and flies from getting in. John listened carefully and tried on every occasion not to do so. However, John did it a few times unintentionally over the 5 years period. He did apologise every time he has done so. Now, John does it again, leaving the wardrobe open in the master bedroom. Maria finds it this time very annoying. She starts a conversation stating that John didn't care about her wishes, and she gets very upset. Because of the most recent experience, Maria believes and emphasises that this time is more important compared to any other. Therefore, she didn't speak to John the whole day. Maria also intensified the discussion compared to the previous times, bringing information from the past and making a general assumption due to the most vivid experience. In other words, remembering the most recent activity, instead of the other occasions when John closed the wardrobes thousands of times before. "You have always been careless, and ignoring my wishes, why are you doing this?!" What could Maria have done better? What about John? Well, she couldn't probably say, "Thank you for leaving the wardrobe open, or remembering the number of times when John closed them off". That's mainly because the action was not lining up with her feelings. Probably, accepting John's negligence from time to time, looking at the overall picture when John closed the wardrobes so many times before. In addition, appreciate the fact that John apologises every time he does so and trying his best not to leave any wardrobe open. Sometimes, we only remember what we think is favourable to us based on the most recent scenario. In most cases, it isn't. It comes naturally as a self-protection mechanism when something gets out of control, endangering the architecture of our own belief system and possibly avoiding getting harmed. Whenever we face such a situation from time to time, what can be done to avoid making inadequate assumptions?

- Before taking a substantial decision, looking at the entire picture can be a good idea, not to reach a decision based only on one off scenarios
- Look into the availability of choices and alternatives
- If a memory comes out too quickly and it's the only one, it's probably not the most appropriate one
- Searching for any evidence to support the decision taken
- Just because it worked well in the past, doesn't necessarily mean it works well this time, especially where something happened with higher emotional impact

Vivid experiences are misinterpreted in the field of the stock market too. During the Black Monday in 1987, the stock market faced an enormous downsize. It was the biggest of its kind in history moving approximately 30 percent in a day. This caused many individuals and corporations a lot of pain where most people became fearful, retracting any funds left in their related investments. Next time when an investment is made based on a single premise, an individual may remember what happened last time. This is mainly because of the most recent activity; an individual weighs more the next event because of what happened in the previous one. What if it happens again?

XII
The role of luck and its probability

"Mother Nature"

From a young age, I have developed an interest in growing plants. I learned from my father when I was six. Nothing more, but garden-fresh tomatoes. I had to pause this interest for several years. In 2021, I decided to try again. I chose cherry tomatoes, which are one of my favourite fruits including their aroma that comes naturally. As a note, all seeds were removed from a cherry tomato that I believed was the most colourful, sweet and ripe at the time. I then selected 4 large pots specifically designed for such activity while dividing the seeds equally in those pots. Throughout the growing process, all tomato plants were exposed to the same conditions from start to finish. This included an identical treatment in terms of light exposure, humidity and soil. In other words, all 4 plants received the same care, with an extremely small variation, if any, in the growing process. For example, using the same soil, separation, tying, pruning, and watering. The timing of the treatment was variable but precise, as all 4 plants were exposed to the same schedule, early morning or late evening, ensuring that all plants followed the same process in the same attempt and session. At the time when tomatoes were ready for eating, something surprising and unexpected showed up. However, this was noticeable slightly earlier in the growing phase, just before the tomatoes began to turn red. One of the plants barely had few tomatoes and didn't turn red yet, another showed significant blossom-end rots, while the last 2 plants flourished with abundant bloom and rich tomatoes. I couldn't find any real explanation. All I said was: That's interesting…! The probability that all four tomato plants to be in a similar way - either ripe or unripe - was quite high, yet the results were highly diversified. Some people may call this effect as 'natural selection', a process where plants survive by becoming more adaptable to change and environment.

Malcolm is in his late 20's. He was able to save some money over the years. Now, he wants to maximise his earnings. He believes that one way to do so is by taking a financial risk and investing 30% of his savings in company 'y'. Not a bad idea! Many people would argue that Malcolm didn't take the best decision due to the poor management, high competitiveness and uncertain future prospects in the sector. He clearly admits his lack of knowledge in the subject, plus he never has done this before. Malcolm closed his eyes and hoped for the best. A year later, he was pleasantly surprised to see that his decision paid off, enjoying an outstanding 150% profit. In comparison, experts with more than 15 years' knowledge in the same field, only benefitted a margin of 12%.

Luck is a fascinating and captivating phenomenon, as there is no formula or pattern developed to obtain or anticipate such a thing. It does not favour anyone in particular or it does someone else higher than average. You only need to try once, or perhaps several thousand times. With that in mind, people who try more regardless of the subject, tend to have a higher chance of success, yet the outcome still remains uncertain. This is what makes it so interesting. Luck works hand in hand with randomness and against the probability theory. Whenever chance favours an individual, they can become lucky or unlucky. Some people attribute luck solely to their personal merit and effort. When an effort is made, luck will follow too. This perspective sounds reasonable, yet it's correlated to the probability outcome, the

The role of luck and its probability

likelihood for something to happen. The higher the chance, the safer the way. However, the contribution of randomness makes it uncertain. No amount of effort, skills and dedication will increase the chance to 100%, or to be certain about something. Many people invest their effort, skills and knowledge to the best they can, but only a fraction seems to yield effective or successful results. Luck comes into various aspects in someone's life, not necessarily based on financial status or success. A few moments of bad luck can transform someone's life. In opposition, a stroke of luck can save considerable time and effort. Factors such as the native place, thinking styles, environment, free of accidents and health conditions, genetic background, natural abilities or the person we share our life with, they all represent a portion of it.

When it comes to probability, it's defined as the number of favourable cases divided by the total number of possible outcomes. For example, when flipping a coin, the probability to show either head or tail is 50%. Then, we can witness a more complicated one, forecasting the weather, how the stock market will perform or even a medical diagnosis. This is because there are many influencing factors involved to calculate such probability. False positives and false negatives are used in medical institutions to deal more efficiently with a diagnosis, and to treat people accordingly.

Tom and James are two dynamic and talented individuals when it comes to their field of profession. They are both specialised in civil engineering, highly qualified with a prestigious degree and several years of experience in the chosen domain. In addition, they have demonstrated enthusiasm, hard work and a high level of intelligence over the years and more importantly a vision where they want to be in the next decade. A few years later, James unexpectedly deals with a health condition. He is unable to fully engage in his profession and must put everything on hold, leading him to take a year off work. Tom contradictorily, sees an opportunity in his role due to his current boss leaving the company. Therefore, he is assigned as the head of the department. For James, it's slightly more challenging to find a leader position in a new company, due to the lack of experience in the field. A few years later, Tom moves up again climbing the corporate ladder and he's now in the position he wanted to be, for example, 5 years ago. Well done, Tom! James, on the other hand, is still engaged in the same work he was doing 5 years ago focusing more on the expertise, rather than management, changing few other companies in between. He had to postpone his aspirations and move everything to a slight extent. He is still very determined though. Tom takes full credit for his achievements and believes that he worked hard and, together with his willingness, have brought him where he wanted to be. He fails to acknowledge the role of luck may have played in his journey. In opposition, James feels extremely lucky to have recovered from his health condition, providing for his family while still being able to pursue his dreams. Getting the right opportunity at the right time plays a significant role in someone's success. If this isn't luck, then what is? Certainly, all the necessary qualities and skills might contribute to their success, yet the luck's role can provide a catalyst that varies from person to person. The former US President Barack Obama expressed his sentiment when it comes to this subject during his 2012 presidential campaign, stating: *"If you get successful and are where you are, you didn't get that on your own, something or someone helped you along the way!"*

When an individual makes a binary decision with a 50% chance of success and it results in a good outcome, they might represent themselves as fully skilled and qualified for that occasion, even in circumstances where the initial decision was not the most appropriate at the time. They tend to overlook the role of luck in the given scenario. Sometimes good decisions lead to a bad outcome and bad decisions lead to a good result, as observed in Malcolm's case. In opposition, well-informed decisions set from the beginning can turn into a bad outcome. This is because something along the way changes, becoming unforeseen and unpredictable. Even if a decision worked well in the past or it was identified as the best practice before, doesn't always work for future cases. However, both examples have something in common, before a decision is made, individuals have the best intentions for it. For example, a couple may decide to purchase a property that initially meets all their criteria. A few months later, a land subsidence that occurred 2 miles away, caused the local area to be vulnerable to flooding. As a note, it has never been previously reported any activity of this kind. Therefore, the house price drops by 25% within a matter of weeks, leading to numerous environmental issues. In another example, consider the process of a startup business. After a year, the business you own shows a good performance with positive prospects too. A few years later, a competitor builds a similar business nearby, 5 times larger, attracting most of the clients. As a consequence, your business shows poor results in trading a year after.

Luck originates from randomness. When it comes to random events, there is no actual prediction or relation between 2 or more samples. These samples are random variables and cannot be represented by any information from the past. For example, choosing something complex, such as national lottery, the way the numbers are selected. In this case, the numbers are chosen randomly. In addition, the selection of these numbers shows no correlation between them, neither for the last 9 nor for the last 900 draws. In the EuroMillions extract, the winning ticket must match the main 5 numbers out of 50, as well as 2 additional numbers from a pool of 12 known as Lucky Stars. To match the first 5, there are 2,118,760 cases available. For the Lucky Stars, 66 combinations. In total, this brings the number of possible cases to 139,838,160. Consequently, there is a chance of winning, 1 to approximately 139millions. Considering the price of a single ticket at £2.50, buying all possible tickets would cost around £349 million. However, there is a small problem, the winning prize is much less than the total spending and you can only hope to be the solely winner with the magic numbers. In this case, you can consider yourself lucky if you hold the winning ticket.

Probability, on the other side, refers to the likelihood for something to occur. It can be assigned to almost anything in this world. This includes the chances of success, find a loving partner, achieving financial comfort, and even on some occasions, life expectancy. Let's consider the following example: In a basket there are 100 small boxes, they all look identical when it comes to appearance, but each box is numbered from 1 to 100. Inside each box is a substantial prize, ranging from £1 to 1 million. The first 10 numbers contain a prize of £1 each. The next 80 numbers of £1000. The numbers between 91 and 100 have a value of a million. Now, suppose person A and B are allowed to pick up twice a box individually. What would be the probability that person B to get at least the prize of 1 million? As a note, when a box is chosen for the first time, the same box will be replaced in the basket to have the same initial conditions for each drawing. On the first attempt, person A extracts the box number 8. The second time, person A picks up the same box number 8. This is what randomness does. Slightly unfortunate for person A. In contrast, person B chooses the box number 99 on the 1st attempt. Person B hasn't done anything different, when it comes to a specific skill set applied. The probability that person A, respectively B, to get at least the prize of a million, is the same. They both had the same chances of picking the high-value box from the beginning. In other words, 10% from their 1st attempt plus another 10% from the second attempt. In total, 19% chance of success. Person A selected the boxes that were the most unfavourable in this case, while person B selected the winning one on their 1st attempt.

Sometimes, regardless of whether the odds are against us or in our favour, it doesn't necessarily mean anything, as randomness plays its part. If you have 90% chance of success and the outcome turns out to be a good one, would you consider yourself lucky? Probably you should...!

Probability	*Success (yes, no)*
Low <10%	Yes – lucky
High >90%	Yes – effort related based?
Low <10%	No – do you even try?
High >90%	No – unlucky
Low <10%	Either Yes/No – pure randomness
High >90%	Either Yes/No – pure randomness

Probability – the normal distribution

Normal distribution is a revolutionary concept in the way something is shown and described by several observations which are generated randomly. The German mathematician, Karl Friedrich Gauss discovered its real magnitude and importance in the 19th century. He realised that when analysing a large set of data points, the graph tends to follow a specific shape often known as the bell curve. For instance, when several random points are spread over a certain time, their distribution in relation to the average number is unknown. That unknown number becomes a random variable. However, when the sample size of observations increases to a larger scale, the average of these variables tends to conform to a normal distribution. For this reason, the graph becomes relatively and under some conditions, normal.

The probability distribution shows how variables are represented by different possible outcomes. A penalty shoot-out is chosen as an example. Suppose we analyse 20 sample shots taken by different players. When a player takes a shot, there are a few options – considering the shots are random from different players. On the 1st attempt from the first player, the ball goes in the top right corner of the target. When the second player takes the shot, the ball is shot to the middle-left quadrant. The ball also hits the crossbar once and it goes outside the goal area, approximately 2 meters to the left. There are occasions when a ball exceeds different margins within the main target. When a small number of shots are observed, in this example 20, each data point represented is not symmetrical to the average number, so the graph observed from the plots does not follow a normal distribution. (Only in one exception that all players would hit the ball approximately in the same spot – extremely unlikely). These points are random to the mean. The mean number is defined by the sample data of how many numbers are used. For instance, the mean number of 8, 5, 4, 9, 3, 6, 5 is 5.7. In the case of penalty shoots, the mean number (in this case it would refer to location) can be found anywhere within or outside the goal, which entirely depends on where most players will hit the ball. However, if the number of data points increases to 1000 or 10,000, their distribution tends to follow a normal distribution. In this scenario, most data points are closer to the mean, while the other points fall on the outer extremes. Under some conditions, there are some exceptions where few points may lie outside the normal distribution curve, often named as 'special causes'. Such anomalies can occur when a player hits the ball inappropriately by accident (e.g. not even reaching the goal or too far from it).

Often referred to as the Gaussian distribution, this shape is commonly found in probability calculations, reflecting patterns in nature or human characteristics. The graph is a statistical tool to analyse random variables that are spread over a certain time period. The distribution not only follows a certain domain and shape, but it also shows how a certain number of data points are represented symmetrically in relation to the average number within a Cartesian coordinate system. Whether we are lucky or not, missing a flight or getting a good night's sleep before the final exam, are just some examples used to observe the frequency of certain outcomes from a specific value, feature or constraint. The applications of normal distribution are vast, ranging from measuring someone's IQ, financial econometrics, and even to studying divorce rates. On these grounds, more frequent observations tend to cluster around the average, while the less frequent ones are farther away from it.

Below are some examples of possible outcomes in various circumstances following a normal distribution, especially when a high number of variables are observed. This is to highlight the importance of such distribution graph when it comes to luck and other areas.

1. Following an unhealthy diet regularly or consuming 'junk food' regularly for the past 15 years
2. The profitability or success rate of a start-up business in the first year of trade (25% or higher)
3. Smoking 20 cigarettes or more every day for the last 25 years
4. The effectiveness of a drug or medication (E.g. antibiotics, antidepressants)

How can I improve my day...?

5. Luck based on effort, skills and merit

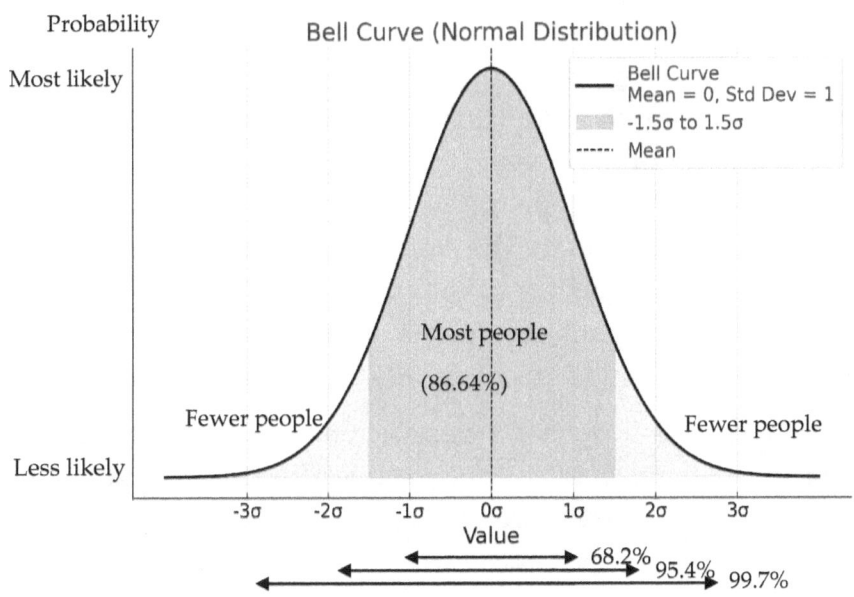

1	Negligible	Unhealthy / overweight	Harmful / critical
2	Successful	Surviving / average performance	Poor performance
3	Healthy	Health deterioration	Life threatening
4	Ineffective	>60% works / average	Deteriorative
5	Lucky	Moderately awarded	Unlucky

In the first year of a start up business, most people show either low-average performance or struggle to survive, despite their high levels of effort, skills and dedication. Fewer people are positioned on the extremes, showing either poor performance (e.g. negative balances, unprofitability) or excellent performance. Similarly, most people who have smoked continuously for 25 years, their health is deteriorating, showing symptoms of lung diseases, dental problems or aging faster than normal. Some people are unaffected by this usage, while some others exhibit critical signs, or life-threatening conditions. In contrast, the effectiveness of antibiotics is significantly higher. A study involving more than 13,000 participants showed a success rate of up to 95%. This leads to a narrowed distribution curve with a smaller standard deviation. Consequently, a smaller percentage of people will be unaffected by it or are immune to the treatment due to previous medication or other factors. Alternatively, approximately 1 in 20 individuals, may experience mild symptoms such as a skin rash or nausea, while 1 in a 1000 can show signs of allergies or swollen areas.

In terms of luck, most people who deserved to be lucky based on their merit and effort, show a moderate result. Luck tends to follow certain trends. Some people are luckier than average, while others more unfortunate. Interestingly, this concept can be flipped, revealing a new perspective. Someone can maintain a healthy diet every day most of their life and can still become unprotected to an unhealthy condition. According to National Public Radio, approximately 36% of United States adult citizens are obese, and around 75% of them claim to have a good nutrition, despite the contrary. In the case of smoking, a non-smoker can still experience symptoms with their lungs or age faster than normal.

These examples generally adhere to a normal distribution curve within their specific domains. Most people fall within 68-86 percentile range, which represents a deviation +-1.5 from the mean. Around 99.7 percent falls within +-3 standard deviations from the average. Various factors and the size of sample data can influence the representation of these distributions. As a result, the farther away from the average number, the fewer people are found. The six standard deviation has an accuracy of 99.9996%.

Approximately 4 cases of a million represent an exception or error.

If more tomato plants were used, the results would most likely have followed a normal distribution curve, where the majority would be rich and blooming, while fewer poorly rooted or vice versa. The outcome was subjected to the environment, seeds quality, and other exposing factors.

XIII
The unknown unknown

On Monday, 6th February 2023, at 04.17, a natural disaster was seen in Turkey. More precisely, an earthquake, in the surroundings of Gaziantep, where more than 50,000 lives were lost during the tragedy. It was the biggest of its kind in that region. One instance of many others, where unpredictability contributed the most to the main event. In 2004, a similar catastrophic scenario occurred in the Indian Ocean, where approximately 230,000 lost their lives along the surrounding coasts. A conventional framework based on the unknown unknown. Location, time, and scale of the event were the 3 most important aspects of the unexpected scenario. There are additional examples, such as 9/11, Russo-Ukrainian War, Brexit, Black Monday, COVID-19 that serve as instances of unidentified events. The core characteristics of human nature distort us to believe that it was easy knowable and predictable from the beginning. Nasim Taleb, a risk analysist, and professor at New York University, describes this type of event as the 'black swan theory'. It's defined by a metaphor when an incident arises as a surprise. In other words, an unexpected event that could happen at any given time. To meet the requirements of a black swan or sometimes described as 'the problem of induction', it must satisfy the following:

- The previous data cannot outline a definite possibility of such event
- It is distinguished by an extreme impact
- Can become understandable after the incident
- We are not informed about the event

When Matthew is seen twice in a row at a specific coffee shop on Sunday morning around 9 a.m., several remarks are made on the principle that Matthew may attend the same place around 9 a.m. every Sunday. When these observations accumulate several times in a row, the assumptions become clearer that Mathew goes for a coffee break every Sunday morning at the same place. Even when a large number of observations are considered, it is still not certain that Matthew will attend the coffee shop every Sunday morning by 9 a.m. This is based entirely on the argument that historical data forecasts the future, which often is considered just an assumption (likely or unlikely). However, there is a high probability that Matthew is seen next Sunday at the coffee shop, but not certain. If the assumption is made based on a large number of observations, but Matthew is absent on a particular Sunday, that situation would create a surprise scenario for those who expect him to be there.

When we make assumptions based on previous data or models, it's important to understand our knowledge of a particular event without concluding that something will happen at a specific time. When it comes to our own awareness, the unknown unknown is part of the 4-quadrant model of knowledge named as Johari window:

1. **The known known.** We are aware of something we know. This model is represented by facts normally. An individual understands a certain area.
2. **The known unknown.** This model refers to the things that we understand but we don't know. Simply, we are aware of something we don't know (a particular area, a subject, or the possession of own abilities). For example, when a flight gets cancelled. We know from time to time that flights may get cancelled, but we don't know if that happens when we travel. Or acknowledging the lack of expertise in a particular subject outside our own circle of competence.

3. **The unknown known.** In this section, an individual is not aware of something they know, but others know about their knowledge or attributes. For instance, we might have hidden qualities that we are not aware of e.g. being a great communicator, good at helping others, honest, or whatever it might be, but instead others tell us. As a remark, an individual is not aware of their aptitudes.

4. **The unknown unknown.** We are not aware of something we don't know or understand. In principle, it tends to be one of a kind scenario where something happens out of the blue and any previous statistical information cannot outline the likelihood of it. Considering the same example with the flight, an unknown unknown scenario would be: 'A flight will get cancelled, but it will never be re-scheduled due to the airline becoming insolvent for the time being'.

Usually, the more uncertain a situation is, the more certain we become in the opposite direction. Before travelling to a destination, it's uncertain that the flight will get cancelled, on the other side we become more certain that the flight will not be cancelled.

There are many other examples, where something unexpected comes into our daily life, not necessarily with a great impact, but instead playing a unique part based on individual premises, as a group or society. Harland Sanders who created KFC at the age of 65 represents one of them, someone's partner wanting to divorce after 20 years of marriage despite the other person not showing any previous signs pointing in that direction, or a car suddenly breaks down on the highway considering it was a brand-new car. These unexpected scenarios usually come as a surprise, often tipping the balance towards negative outcomes. They tend to be unpredictable, uncertain that something will happen or never happened previously. How should we act or prepare in advance for something we never experienced before? We think we know...but the reality can be entirely different when we experience it in real time. For example, going through a divorce for the first time, especially if it comes by surprise, how should we respond in this context? When this happens, we often try to protect ourselves with self-curing and self-justifying thoughts such as: "They did not deserve me, they will regret their decision, I hope they will feel the same I do", often failing to observe our own faults, our own behaviour that contributed to the situation. At the same time, it could be the other way around, feeling remorseful, responsible and wishing we could have done things differently. Perhaps, it's essential to adopt a more sustainable behaviour, reflecting on the real contributions from both sides and using it as an experience to learn and to grow. Second time will be different. Hopefully!

Something certain about life is that life itself is uncertain, and changes are unavoidable. A change in time, environment or personal wellbeing. Some people describe these unexpected events, the beauty of uncertainty - the not knowing. No one has a crystal ball where they can see the future with preciseness and accuracy. At least not as far as I know. In general, opinions are divided, where some people experience difficult emotions and feeling 'scratchy' when dealing with uncertainty. They often crave assurance and security, following a certain plan to achieve their goals. In these situations, the uncertainty disrupts the architecture of any plan or viewpoint. As a result, people tend to use worrying as an approach to forecast the future and to avoid any unpleasant surprises.

In general, mostly everything we do on a regular basis comes with an implication, whether it's crossing the street, driving from A to point B, flying out and so on. Normally, we don't think about the risks and consequences associated with those. We take an action without any sort of reasoning effort.

It becomes a normality. Basically, we integrate those risks and consequences into our daily routine. When an effort to manage any of those becomes too strong or deep, problems can arise. We often deal with discomfort or worries consistently, while trying to emphasise our attention on something that creates safety. For better or worse, certainty gives people a sense of control, what they can do or change in a particular subject. Surely, there are many aspects that can be controllable such as our actions or whether we choose to show up. On many other occasions, things that are uncontrollable, the meteorological conditions, other people's opinions and actions, or the future. However, some of these factors can be influenced to some 'extent'. For example, if someone lives in a rainy and cloudy place, they might choose to relocate to a warmer and sunnier place, not as in the weather can be controllable.

The uncertainty cannot be eliminated from our lives. The more we try to eliminate it, the worse it often becomes, as we will be exposed intensively to worries when there is no need most of the time. Fortunately or unfortunately, nothing in this world can be guaranteed, whether it's the person we share our life with, personal wellbeing, financial situation, or what lies ahead. A way to deal with uncertainty, is to cultivate tolerance. It would be foolish not to consider it from time to time. Sometimes, changing a belief or attitude isn't something that we can switch on and off with ease. It requires a high cognitive effort to tolerate a new idea or concept while remaining honest with ourselves. Once this is done, it becomes easier and easier. Dealing with the unknown unknown or something we never experienced before, how can we prepare in advance? E.g. during a natural disaster, a pandemic, the death of a loved one, a critical health condition and so on. The experience itself will often teach us how to handle such scenarios, as well as the lessons and approaches from previous experiences.

XIV
The ability to unlearn

Living in a fast-paced environment where information grows at an unprecedented rate, we continuously have the tendency to acquire a diverse set of skills and dedicating ourselves to various activities to become better at. This approach can be a practical way to meet our needs and desires. This is especially critical in a competitive landscape, as we aim to keep up with the latest trends. As a result, we often engage in various learning courses or strive on the career path to enhance both curriculum vitae and personal development. For example, participating in various educational programs, pursuing a higher education, or developing strategies that align with and support a business objective, can be beneficial. This focus on specialisation enhances the chances of success, improves employability, and adds value both to individuals and their organisations.

That's not always the case. Achieving personal goals or increasing the chances of success doesn't always depend only on learning new information. An important factor is our ability to unlearn what we've previously learned. This process of unlearning can more challenging than acquiring new knowledge. Of course, learning is essential, regardless of its quality and type. For example, to improve our language or communication skills, an effective approach is to unlearn the unnecessary words that we have accumulated over time, especially when they no longer serve a purpose. In other words, identifying the 'bad apples' from a basket and put them to one side. Forget about them or throw them in the rubbish bin. It sounds easy, no? Well, it is not that uncomplicated. When it comes to improving vocabulary, knowing less words while trying to improve those is often more beneficial than knowing more words that cannot be applied appropriately.

Over the years, we are exposed to countless notions and ideas we like to 'explore'. For example, trying a savoury dessert after a meal, purchasing items that we only use once and never again, watching a variety of TV shows, engaging in lengthy conversations - related and unrelated, or simply browsing the internet. At the time, these activities can feel good, relaxing or enjoyable. Due to their high frequency, these activities can turn into habits. Therefore, we often engage in a specific action or reasoning without effort. To break, stop or pause some of these habits can be extremely challenging. Same applies to unlearning some that we've become masters of, especially something that has been used for a long time in our routines.

At first glance, the idea of unlearning something seems slightly negative. It's like moving backwards rather than forwards. At the same time, using this approach can significantly enhance our resilience and allows us to overcome different challenges with a more open mindset. Many of these habits are deeply imprinted in our mind, often without us even realising it. Certainly, we don't have a switch "off" button that would allow us to delete them instantly. It's much harder to unlearn something than to learn it in the first stage. As we age, the idea of disrupting patterns that have been developed over the years becomes even more challenging. Some of these habits are not just activities but also thinking patterns or responses throughout the days. The more we encounter these habits, the more difficult it becomes to eliminate them from our lives. Perhaps, they may not completely be deleted from our mind, but we can replace them with more effective ways of thinking. This shift will allow us to become more adaptable to new experiences and changes. Science supports this too, that it can be done. The conscious mind together with its flexibility and ability to think carefully whenever an important decision must be made can often make this feasible. The brain stores it as a memory in the background, for the good causes in case the individual may need it at a later time. The process of unlearning often involves something new that becomes dominant. This reduces the effect of the old configuration. With time, the old configuration tends to fade way while creating more space for the new information, experiences and thinking patterns. The time is unknown, variable. Unlearning is also based on something that becomes outdated and requires a change while no longer serves a purpose. Of course, this cannot be accomplished with ease, it takes awareness, time, effort, discomfort and willingness to adapt to both, old configuration and new one. Additionally, whenever we are challenged with such requests, it's important to change the scenery, what we see and experience. For example, challenge our perceptions, changing the place we live, social groups and interactions. The shift in surroundings often creates new challenges that expose us to different ideas and thinking patterns.

Olivia, a mother of two in her mid-50s, has been happily married for over 25 years. During her last medical check-up, she learned that she needs to pay more attention to her health to prevent deterioration, particularly in terms of her diet and exercise. While she is not overweight, Olivia admits that she has not maintained the best lifestyle regarding physical activity or nutrition. This pattern has been evident since her teenage years, as she has consistently indulged in rich meals and desserts. For many years, Olivia felt lost in her daily routine, as many of us do. Can she overcome or unlearn those unhealthy eating habits she has developed over the years? This requires additional thought. Reasoning that it can be hard - can be helpful, reasoning that it can be easy – can be difficult. Obviously, she can try, that's probably the best thing she can do. With that in mind, she must recognise that the habits she formed over the years might be deeply ingrained and won't be easily changed. Leaving something to the last minute, falling into deceitful patterns, and becoming easily resentful are just a few examples of the habits that can become part of a daily routine.

Wolfgang Dürheimer, former president of Porsche AG in the research and development, used this concept to the best of his ability. From a young age, Wolfgang discovered his passion in the motorsport industry and aspired to become a professional racer. After several years, he remarkably realised that he could practise day and night, he was unable to reach where he wanted, in the top cohort. He realised that to achieve something, passion and hardworking is not enough. As a result, he shifted his attention to the technological side in the same industry, aiming to make an impact throughout vehicle creation rather than racing. Wolfgang Dürheimer remained in history with his outstanding career when he was in charge as the president of Bugatti Automobile in 2017, producing the fastest car on record. The model was able to achieve a top speed of 261miles per hour, identified as the 'Everest' in the internal combustion engines.

In essence, we often engage in certain habits without even being aware of them. Some of these habits can give us a sense of reward, pleasure or a good feeling. Sometimes, emotions can take over our reasoning, causing to ignore the long-term consequences of our actions. What feels good now, might not be at a later time. Can they be prevented? They definitely can, although we may not recognise the need for change until it's too late.

XV
Improving the day...

Mostly every day comes with an opportunity to change for better. What specific actions and decisions are to be made to reach such expected outcome? What can we truly do at the time? An effective improvement on a large scale with a great impact cannot be accomplished in just one day. More days are needed. In the number of hundreds, thousands or even more. With that in mind, every day brings its own benefits, which contributes to the overall result. Each day works as a foundation. It gives us the opportunity to live to our full potential, not just in the present but also in the future. To see an improvement on a large scale over time, an attention is needed to focus on each day as it arrives. For example, identifying the decisions which are within our abilities and taking an action towards any improvements that can be accomplished, regardless of how insignificant the effect is. Of course, we must not forget the past, as it's part of who we are, giving us the idea to uphold the difference between a bad day and an effective one. The future is equally important, offering a sense of purpose and direction in the present moment based entirely on the choices and opportunities we encounter each day. A decision will be influenced by our emotional state, thoughts, memories, and the environment in context with others at that specific time. Those decisions made can guide our destiny and shape our future.

There are countless improvements that can be made on a daily basis. In this book, many contributions were highlighted on how a day can be improved. For example, throughout happiness, gratitude, self-awareness, challenging and difficult situations, performance and many more in between. Relying only on impulses and intuitions as we go along? Sometimes, that's the best thing we can do. To reach quick decisions and conclusions leading to a favourable result. Yet, most times if we don't know where we are, I believe it would represent a challenging task to do so. A good approach is to acknowledge where we currently 'stand'. In other words, recognising our own routines, behaviour, ideas, thinking styles, flaws, distractions, distortions, or decision-making process. Admitting to ourselves what we could have done better, if the outcome was good - why it was good, if the outcome was poor - why it was poor. Of course, there is not enough time to reflect over everything we do on a daily basis, but we want to do it in a more sensible way. It wouldn't be productive otherwise. Allowing to make errors is another valuable concept representing an opportunity for an improvement rather than reaching the near impossible, striving for perfection and setting extremely high expectations. We are more likely to achieve a resolution that works for us and it's realistic. According to a YouGov national survey, approximately 1 in 4 people abandon their initial goals due to one of these reasons. Just because something didn't follow our plans, should we be resentful or perhaps looking forward to such opportunity? I suppose there is one way to find out…

An improvement in any aspect of life is a continuous cycle. Whether it's professionally, financially, well-being related and so on. This is applicable for both – on individual basis and as a bond. It continuously changes as we go along. It cannot entirely be finished or fully accomplished. Good enough is good enough, on that day, at that moment in time; just to acknowledge as long as something was better compared to few months or even few years ago. Even when something leaves room for improvement that would represent an opportunity for an improvement. For example, if you get an A instead of A*. Should you be disappointed that you didn't get an A*? Perhaps you should, or you shouldn't.

Every so often, most of us require doing something right the first time without further attempts. How feasible is this in context to the given time? Occasionally, there is only one shot available within a specific subject, wishing to make the best of it. However, it may end up with an unfavourable result. For example, during an interview process where a candidate is not nominated, missing a penalty kick in the final game, a surgeon makes an error leading to someone's death or perhaps a leader takes a financial decision causing a business to become insolvent. When this happens, people wish to go back in time to change something or show signs of remorse. Unfortunately, this is not possible for the first instance. In the second case, this is to be expected from time to time. It comes with life's opportunities and the likelihood for something to happen. For better or worse, the end result lay in the decisions made since an action was needed at the time. We hope next time to be different. Depending on various circumstances, sometimes, not everything requires an action, a decision at the time. Pausing an action can be identified as a good approach. For example, if I don't do x and y – I am going to miss out this great opportunity. This can also translate into, 'I will fail if don't grab the benefits that come with this opportunity'. Other examples are also considered: taking a big financial decision when emotions are on the extreme spectrum, or perhaps during times of uncertainty.

Whenever exposed to various problems or challenges, if the result is not in our favour, doesn't necessarily mean it's a bad day. It generates a comparison to understand what a good day really is. We can use that day as a lesson to understand what went wrong and try to avoid a similar scenario in the future. Furthermore, switching between different neural oscillations throughout the day can be beneficial, make better choices and swift responses based on what can be accomplished at the time. For example, when we are in theta phase (with a lower frequency range) that requires our methods and thinking approaches to solve a problem, would take significantly longer than usual as it would occur in the gamma phase. In other words, cooperating with ourselves, along with the environment and what the day may offer at the time. Similarly, during an emotional state, where we are more likely to find errors whenever a situation demands so.

We can also try to avoid something that deteriorate the day. Things that normally do not help us. Blaming others, waiting for miracles to happen, or full of bitterness, especially when something didn't go follow the plan and errors are found. In this case, responsibility and accountability work hand in hand to promote a self-growth mindset and trust. On these grounds, errors and mistakes can be changed. Hopefully for better. This is first applicable on the individual basis and eventually as a bond.

Throughout the day, sometimes we are exposed to a hard 'point'. A point that may seem unmanageable at the time. This 'point' refers to a situation that becomes overwhelming and highly strained. For instance, if you attempt to run a certain distance, after a while you may find it extremely difficult to continue. Taking a break or even a sense of abandonment are converted into real options. On the other hand, once passing that stage, there are times where the journey becomes easier.

Most of our days are repeated functions. Approximately 95% of the time we think and act in the same way as in the previous day, with no major changes in between. Thus, most days are lost in routine, a routine which eventually become a pattern. The way we showed up today will be no different from tomorrow's.

Research supports this information too. In 2005, the National Science Foundation stated that an average person has regularly the same thoughts, feelings and how they see their life every day. With that in mind, this information can either help us or hold us back. An improvement lies in these thoughts and actions because they are predominantly used at a high frequency. Identifying or not identifying patterns that seem to work in our routine can be fundamentally important to improve ourselves. Things that we want to do more or less of, depending on certain activities. This creates a possibility to interrupt or reinforce a thought, an action, respectively a judgement. A day can be divided into smaller fragments. This can be further categorised into a standard and non-standard working day. Based on 24 hours available in a standard working day, where and how do we spend most of the time? We can start with the following:

- Sleeping
- Morning routine
- Eating, a few times a day
- Driving to work and any other activities
- Working
- Showering, dressing, undressing
- Household tasks, parenting duties
- Rest, rejuvenation, reading
- Exercising
- Cooking, shopping
- Distractions (unnecessary discussions, inquires, phone calls, checking the news, social media, etc)

Once all these activities are added up based on the average time considered for each one, there isn't much time left, even when some of them can be done simultaneously. If we are lucky, we get one or two hours. In this timeframe lies opportunities of any kind. It offers a possibility to do something we like. Of course, we must not forget, if something offers an opportunity, at the same time it represents a possibility for a drawback or disappointment. We can go deeper into greater details if we want to. For example, how many hours should I sleep to be effective? Various research studies recommend that an adult should sleep between 7 and 8 hours per day to stay alert and focused the next. Anything more or less, with time, can decrease productivity and reaction time. How much time does someone need for a morning routine to be able to 'wake up'? In other words, resetting after the recovery mode, staying alert while planning for the day ahead. It can take anywhere from 30 minutes to two hours. The time varies widely based on the wishes or activities that are encountered individually.

With that in mind, this routine is highly dependent on the individual's age, marital status, a parent for one or more children, a demanding job and so on. Since we become aware of how and where we spend our time, it increases the chance to develop improvements that might be needed at the time. Breaking a pattern once or from time to time doesn't change much the overall picture. For example, if you work 15h in a day followed by 8 days of inactivity, doesn't mean you are a hard-working person, especially when this is evaluated based on the first few days. Same applies if you lost control and yelled at someone once, doesn't suggest you are a hostile person. The opposite applies if someone initiates an act of kindness once and the list continues. The majority of actions referenced by a time frame can define the end conclusion. Alternatively, skipping good patterns that seem to work in the daily routine (healthy diet, good sleep, exercising) can sometimes be identified as a challenge to cultivate resilience.

Theory vs Practice

Another important way to a self-improvement approach is to distinguish the difference between theory and practice. In this context, the term 'practice' is referred as transforming what we know and what we learn in real world scenarios. Before a situation occurs, some of the perceptions and perspectives we hold prior to that event are often different compared to when something is experienced in real time. For example, when we hold an over-optimistic approach: *'I can do this easily and doesn't take a lot of time too.'* When the real time comes, the outcome is often different from the one we estimated initially. We might find it challenging at times, due to various influential factors, hidden or unfamiliar information. Or simply it becomes harder contrary to the way we expected to be, effortless and timeless. The way something is anticipated, our rich thoughts together with a positive approach do not help us. Of course, it can also happen the other way around, considering something to be difficult and challenging, yet when it's time to implement these ideas, we find it easier than the initial reasoning. With that in mind, the way we show up prior to an event is different from the real time. A sensible way is not to be exposed to the opposite spectrum unless the initial premises set from the beginning demand so, high satisfaction or high disappointment. A large factor contributing to this gap is our emotional state, which often becomes stronger than the reason itself. At the same time, one can be involuntary misrepresented for another. We think we know exactly what we should do, yet actions are still not on the same line with the initial reasoning approach. More specifically, we are not able to act in the way we wanted, whether it feels good or bad, even when our initial reasoning approach suggests otherwise. Emotions can direct how we interpret something while our reasoning approach instantly influences the way we feel.

When it comes to learning, no book, professor or institution tells us what we should do in a particular case, how to effectively deal with certain scenarios when things don't follow the main plan or criteria. We are taught in a standardised scenario, in an ideal situation. Anything else, we have to learn by ourselves and in context to others. We hope that lessons and experiences made over the years can help us manage such scenarios. Sometimes, even those are not much of help when something is observed for the first time. In that case, knowing in advance what we should do, a situation might be different when we experience it by ourselves based on the environment at the time and in context to others. Some of these situations underline a non-linear concept within the society we live in. For example, in a group or collective, an outcome cannot be entirely understood by paying attention to each person individually. A new emergent characteristic can derive from each interaction within their individuals as a group but not present within the individual actions. For instance, a jury's conclusion can show up as a surprise, because the group develops a new decision that cannot be influenced only on individual basis. In terms of the GDP growth, price underlying factors and movements cannot be induced from individual activities, but as a collective.

Moreover, the difference between theory vs practice concept relies on various influential factors and hidden information. The nature of a project, how we show up during an experience, and the group dynamics are just a few of them. For example, a verification test didn't meet its initial specifications – so mostly everything has to start from square one. Someone suddenly loses interest in a project, while two of the team members get off sick, at the same time. Or due to a recent health condition, mostly everything has to be postponed or assigned to someone else. The list continues further when a problem arrives on Friday afternoon when almost everyone has switched off from work and prepared for the weekend. Of course, if this happens several times, it becomes familiar. We tend to learn from it. Another example applies through the theory of 'active listening'. This idea is based on a communication method where attention is necessary, trying to understand without interruption and showing interest by asking appropriate questions. In reality, this concept is often interrupted way too early.

The Tree Swing Analogy

This analogy originates from 1970s when different departments interpreted something else when it comes to the quality of a project management. With time, the tree swing analogy became more and more common in a product development, particularly when project expectations and objectives didn't follow their initial plan. In addition, when a project turned out to be unsuccessful, poorly performed or even failed. A real explanation might be due to the project goals, which constantly change and develop all along within a schedule. Some of the important features set from early stages, become no longer important after a while.

Improving the day...

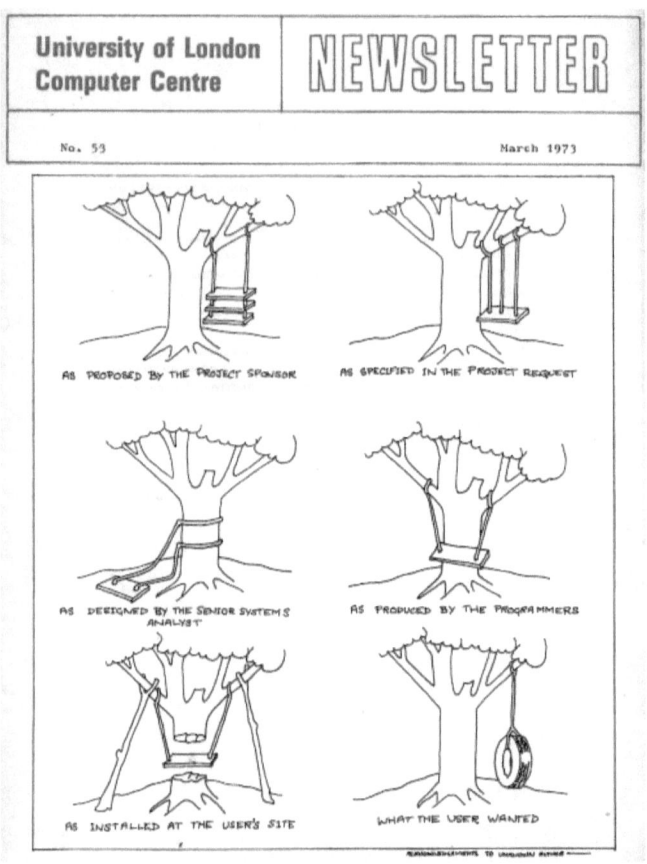

The Swing Tree Analogy
University of London Computer Science No 53, March 1973

The analogy also illustrates the lack of effective communication within multi-disciplinary teams and how something is understood especially during a fast-paced environment. Furthermore, it shows a perception gap between cross-functional teams, as it became more widespread in companies' circles. In other words, how a message is supported and understood through different ways of communication, either by us or by the group dynamics. It relates to the concept of understanding. The process of selecting information and drawing up conclusions between a thought that guides a line of reasoning. For example, the use of premises or sentences followed by a conclusion to draw up a connection between those. This is referred to as an argument. Not as a line of debate between two persons, shouting at each other or contracting, but in a sense of how a conclusion was reached based on the initial premises. Therefore, an argument is valid, invalid, strong, weak, sound and unsound based on how the connection between a set of premises and conclusion is supported. In addition, an argument gives a sentence meaning. *'Good'* arguments are essential in everyday life. To solve problems, to make better choices or decisions in discrete circumstances. They can make a difference between false perspectives we may hold at the time, conflicting claims and judgmental errors. Arguments are fundamental concepts that initially were observed by the ancient Greeks. This was to challenge different theories based on a suspending judgement and discover truths in real life. Arguments are used as an exchange reason along with a conclusion either to weaken or strengthen a theory.

There are different categories of arguments in the realm of reasoning:

- ***Deductive.*** 'All residents of England have free healthcare. Sophie is English, so she has free healthcare.' In a deductive argument, normally there are 2 or more premises followed by a conclusion. Validity and soundness are evaluation properties used to describe the logical structure and the truth of an argument. This example represents a valid and sound argument because both premises and conclusion are true. However, it's possible to have a single premise followed by a conclusion. 'All people are human, therefore I am human'. A deductive argument is a logical structure and becomes valid if the premises are true then the conclusion must also be true. In addition, the conclusion should follow the premises but doesn't necessarily require the premises to be true. A premise offers the reason for believing the truth of the conclusion. A valid argument doesn't determine the truth in reality between those. Can still include a false conclusion implied from a false premise. Furthermore, a valid argument is established in a way that a false conclusion cannot follow both true premises. A sound argument infers a valid argument only if the premises are true. Therefore, in a sound argument the conclusion is guaranteed to be true for all cases.

'Every rectangle has 4 right angles of 90 degrees each. This shape is rectangular, so the sum of all interior angles is 360 degrees'. This is a valid and a sound argument.

'Every rectangle has 4 right angles of 75 degrees each. This shape is rectangular, so the sum of all interior angles is 300 degrees'. This is still a valid argument because the conclusion still follows the premises, but unsound, because one of the premises is false.

An invalid argument can also occur when both premises and conclusion are true individually. 'The grass is green. Rome is the capital of Italy. Therefore, Basset Hound is a dog breed'. Both premises and the conclusion are individually true, but there is no logical structure between them.

Let's look at another example: 'Gregory is human. Some humans live in New York. Therefore, Gregory lives in New York'. This is not a valid argument even when both premises are separately true, because the conclusion didn't logically follow the premises, therefore is an unsound argument. Just because Gregory is human doesn't automatically mean he lives in New York. Validity in a deductive argument does not indicate the truth in reality. It represents the logical structure between premises followed by a conclusion. Alternatively, a sound argument ensures the truth of a conclusion. A deductive argument is used in real applications to solve problems and support decision-making.

Example of an invalid argument between a combination of false premises and true conclusion and true premises and a false conclusion. 'If it's raining, the grass is wet. The grass is wet; therefore it's raining.' Someone could have sprayed it, used sprinkles or due to morning dew.

A deductive argument cannot be defined by a single conditional statement, unless additional premises are used to infer a conclusion. A valid deductive argument comes under different logical forms:

- *Modus Ponens.* 'If premise then conclusion, premise therefore conclusion'. If today is Monday, then I will go to work. Today is Monday, therefore I will go to work. An example of a valid deductive argument following the Modus Ponens, but unsound using this form. 'If I work hard and smart then I am wealthy. I work hard and smart, therefore I am wealthy'. (can be inherited or favoured by luck). Either the premise or conclusion is not 100% only for the two reasons).

- *Modus Tollens.* 'If premise, then conclusion. Not premise, therefore not conclusion'. 'If I am late, then I miss the bus: I am not late, therefore I didn't miss the bus'.

- *Disjunctive syllogism.* 'Premise or conclusion. Not Premise, therefore conclusion'. I am either asleep or awake. I am not awake; therefore I am asleep. A cat is natively either purple or white. This cat is not white, therefore is purple.

This is still a valid argument, but unsound due to its false premise (purple).

- *Syllogism.* 'All premises are X. F is a Premise, therefore F is an X'. All my clothes are dried out. The jumper is a cloth; therefore the jumper is dried out.

- *Deontic logic.* 'Lying is wrong; therefore we must not lie'. This is based on the principle that once we believe lying is wrong, we should believe at the same time, that we should not do it. It doesn't imply that we will not do it. This represents the concept of the things that we should do or not, logically, instead of the question of what is good or bad. If I perform action A, then I need to perform action B. I perform action A, therefore I need to perform B. If I talk to my partner, then I must tell them the truth. I am talking to my partner; therefore I am telling them the truth. Obligation, authorisation, or prohibition are normative models used in this type of argument.

- **Inductive.** This is a form of argument that uses particular premises to draw up a conclusion to create patterns. It relies on evidential support to make future predictions. Unlike deductive arguments, an inductive argument allows room for error, becoming highly probable, but not certain. A conclusion might be true in most cases but not guaranteed in all possible cases. 'Every dog I've played with is friendly. Therefore, all dogs are friendly'. 'I have never seen a black swan till now, so all swans must be white'. In these cases, general assumptions are drawn from the previous observations provided. The evaluation for this type of argument is either strong or weak, depending on how well the conclusion is supported by the premises.

- ***Abductive.*** An argument that implies a conclusion to infer the most likely hypothesis to support the premises. More precisely, it offers the best explanation between the two. In this case, the argument cannot be said with certainty to be true, even the other explanations seem less likely. For example, 'A patient has consistent abdominal pain, so they have appendicitis'. 'Anna is late. She finished her schedule during peak times, so she must be stuck in traffic'. In these situations, an abductive argument cannot be said with certainty to be true, even if the conclusion supports the premise with the most logical observed fact.

- ***Analogical.*** It infers similarities between a premise and a conclusion. As a result, a conclusion is observed based on those premises throughout comparison. 'This project is comparable to the previous one, where budget and timing was shortened, so the outcome should be the same – unrealistic'. 'Every German manufacturing car I owned in the last 10 years was reliable, so Audi is a reliable car'. In real examples, such arguments are applied to solve problems in a new area when information was observed previously in a similar area. The number of similarities or dissimilarities of how a conclusion was drawn can determine the outcome of the argument.

By definition, all the other arguments except deductive are considered unsound because their conclusions do not guarantee certainty for all possible cases, even when the premises are true. Inductive, abductive and analogical arguments allow room for errors. Validity and soundness are applied only to deductive arguments. A sound argument measures the certainty of the logical structure between premises and conclusion, while the other types of arguments measure probability between those. Yet, the evaluation criteria for these types are different such as strong or weak, highly probable and less probable. They are based on the principle of how well the conclusion supports the premises or how the truth of the premises increases the likelihood for the conclusion to be true. Inductive, abductive and analogical arguments are often used in real applications (law, finance, science etc) to create scenarios and draw assumptions due to incomplete information or based on what was observed previously.

In general, the premises used in an argument, do not establish a cause-and-effect association with the conclusion, but instead a logical support or evidence. Using a series of statements followed by a conclusion in an argument can often lead to many errors in the reasoning approach, steering people to reach poor assumptions and decisions based on what was observed at the time.

Circular arguments known as fallacies arguments first appear to be valid, but do not offer a good reasoning. This type of argument refers to the same idea that is used between the premise and conclusion, aiming to validate itself. The form of circular arguments is as follows: *'Premise is true because of the conclusion. Conclusion is true because of the premise.'* In principle, when it comes to this type of argument, its explanation begs the question in a cycle offering no real evidence between the two, between the premise and conclusion. Therefore, a circular argument is considered invalid.

E.g. 'The recent released film is best to watch due to its high recommendation. It's highly recommended because is the best to film to watch.'

'Thomas cannot find a job because he doesn't have experience in the field. He doesn't have experience in the field because he cannot find a job.'

'Warren Buffett is the CEO of Berkshire Hathaway because he is a good leader. He is a good leader because he is the CEO of Berkshire Hathaway.'

'Poor' arguments are frequently observed in the society we live in, whether in group dynamics, workplaces, or personal relationships. Thus, a decision is more expected to be reached based on those arguments, on how well they are supported. We are more likely to make a decision whenever clarity and closeness are in line with each other, and favourable to us. When these factors are further apart, the blurrier something becomes. This leads to unreasonable conclusions and judgements. If something resonates with what we consider important and valuable, we are more inclined to make appropriate adjustments. Sometimes, the evaluation of an argument is not always easily defined and described between a premise and a conclusion. Nor between clarity and closeness. We often form evaluations or judgements even before something is presented to us. A number of previous occurrences can shape our responses, so we know in 'advance' how to handle the situation this time. Or simply because we already 'feel' whether or not something makes sense, regardless of the evidence provided. Several factors can influence the quality of arguments that impact our decision-making. Limited time to make accurate observations, individual interpretations, and the pressure to conform are some examples.

XVI
Preferring a nice lie over the difficult truth...

Two political parties are prepared to run a campaign for a new election. For the purpose of this context, I will call them, party a, respectively party b. When choosing which option is the most appropriate for the job, we are usually exposed to 2 of the most important alternatives - either the leader for party a or b.

Which of the following would you choose?

- The leader of party a revealing: *"It's time for a change, I am going to change x, y, z, fixing all the problems that the people need right now if you vote for me and together, we will find a new way to success."* In simple terms, promising something people want to hear.

- The leader of party b stating perhaps a more honest affirmation: *"I am going to try my best to deliver in the new campaign focusing on x, y, z but probably no major changes are brought up with it."*

In general, no major changes are forecasted regardless of whom is elected. At least, those are not visible to the general population. Why are we more likely to choose the leader from party a instead of b? Amongst the general population, choosing party 'a' comes with a higher probability. So too, the disappointment. Usually, there is a tendency not to deliver all the actions mentioned in their initial statement.

Why are we subjected to such scenarios? I believe it sounds more encouraging and optimistic to the human ear, presenting a clear strategy for upcoming challenges. It feels inspiring and uplifting. However, this does not guarantee a good outcome. While phrase 'a' is presented in a way that is comforting and decorative, at the same time it allows us to avoid confronting the reality, which can sometimes be unpleasant and painful. One reason behind this exposure is the environment we live in, which often encourages us to maintain a positive outlook. Phrase like "If you are positive with a contribution of great effort, everything will be possible" is commonly heard. However, I believe this concept is open to debate. Many people genuinely try their best and put in significant effort, yet only a small percentage appears to achieve their desired outcomes. In essence, those results depend on a wide range of influencing factors. Positivity or optimism holds many advantages such as believing that something will happen or staying motivated during an event. However, we want to do it in a SMART way in relation to one's competence (Specific, Measurable, Achievable, Realistic, and Time-related) rather than on the false premises. While it would increase the likelihood of success, the final outcome will still remain uncertain.

Nick and Jacqueline have been living together for a few years now, enjoying each other's company. In a few days, they plan to attend the wedding of a family friend whom they both have known for decades. They want to put in extra effort when choosing their outfits for this special occasion, as it's an important day for their friend - and for them, since they haven't had the chance to dine out for some time. As they prepare to leave the house, Jacqueline asked Nick if she looks okay and if there is anything about her outfit that needs changing or adjusting. She partly did so because she wanted her look to complement Nick's outfit. It was thoughtful of Jacqueline as she prepared for the evening. Nick quickly responded: "Honey, you look so beautiful; you don't need to change anything!"

However, she pressed him again, revealing her true feelings, "Please don't flatter me; tell me the truth." This time, Nick with no hesitation replied, "Well, the shoes don't match your dress nor my outfit." An hour passed as she tried on different shoes, but they were either uncomfortable or the wrong colour. This led to her growing irritation, and she blamed Nick for their lateness. Frustrated, Jacqueline didn't want to attend the party any longer. "Why did you have to say you didn't like my shoes?" she asked. Nick responded, "my initial intention was to share a compliment, nothing else, yet you refused to accept it. Why did you ask me twice if you didn't want to hear the answer?" Eventually, the tension eased, while both happily attended their friend's party.

What could Nick and Jacqueline have done better?

Nick's initial statement was probably intended to leave the house quickly, as he was aware that this situation had occurred several times before. If this was his motivation, it could be considered slightly selfish. On the other hand, Jacqueline sought a second affirmation waiting for Nick's validation instead of addressing his first comment. However, it was thoughtful of her to ask Nick concerning her dress. In an interview process, the situation is often similar. More frequently than not, an applicant gets the job because they are the most prepared, not because they are the best candidate in that specific role. Furthermore, interviewers may find themselves drawn to what they want to hear, often favouring enthusiasm and eagerness over qualifications and experience. This can lead to a dissatisfaction from both parties the candidate and the employer, resulting in high employee turnover.

Every day often comes with warnings and alarm bells. Being too straightforward with someone you love can shatter them into millions of pieces. While your intention may come from love and your desire for their well-being, family members or close friends sometimes advice you what's best for them rather than your own circumstances, often without realising it. In some cases, being honest with a loved one may not represent the best approach. Opinions are spread differently on this matter. Honesty or truth can cause pain and upset, even when it seems like constructive feedback. This is largely due to individual's perspectives of such discussions, as they can bring back old memories while highlighting something wrong or hurtful, often involving an acknowledgment of one's mistakes that might have been avoided.

Imagine you are invited to dinner at a family friend's home on a Sunday evening. A friend who dedicates significant time and effort to cooking. When it comes to taste, dinner's choices may not resonate with your personal flavour; it's outside your preferences. If asked about your thoughts on the dinner, you might want to think twice about it. If you say: "The dinner is nice, but it doesn't match my taste," may cause a different reaction.

Can the other person benefit from your honesty? They certainly can. It largely depends on the specific situation and various influencing factors such as personal perception, personality, and environment. It's important to recognise that one idea cannot serve as a standardised method which applies to every context; the answer isn't simply yes or no. It would be unwise to claim that a single concept applies to all scenarios. In a medical context, this consideration becomes even more pronounced. For example, if you are a parent who discovers that your 7-year-old child has a serious medical condition, would you choose to tell them the truth? This decision could have various effects on the child. Protection, consideration, encouragement, and witnessing someone's pain are the core influencing factors. Decent honesty is not always considered a good idea. Sometimes, being honest involves the delicate act of sparing someone's feelings. For instance, "Is it a good idea to be truthful with your children about Santa Claus?" Revealing the truth might ruin the magic and spirit... However, each family has the right to choose how they approach this decision, often influenced by their own upbringing. Similarly, if a friend gets married, would you tell them about a small accident involving a close relative that occurred far away on the same wedding day? This situation raises the question of whether sharing such news is appropriate.

In general, promoting one's own interests through lies at the expense of others is a form of deception and considered harmful. Lying can diminish trust and damage interpersonal relationships. People often engage in such circumstances to avoid punishment, while at the same time it can represent a way to protect someone you love. In opposition, being open about your perceptions avoids the need to recall specific details later on, whether it's today, tomorrow, or two years from now.

XVII
The inversion approach

Frequently in life, some problems and challenges cannot be answered or solved in one direction. We should look at them from a different angle, not only forwards but also backwards. This approaching technique is called inversion. In one of the remarkable speeches back in 1986 at Harvard, Charlie Munger, the vice-president of Berkshire Hathaway at the time said: "It is remarkable how much long-term advantage people like us have gotten by trying constantly avoiding being foolish rather than seeking to be very intelligent." This thinking tool was initially inspired by the German mathematician Carl Gustav Jacob Jacobi in 1829. He participated and contributed to numerous scientific problems in algebra, such us elliptic functions, differential equations, and number theory, where particularly he was recognised to solve complex problems using the following approach technique 'man muss immer umkehren', meaning 'invert, always invert'. Carl Jacobi realised that a new, easier way to solve problems is when you turn them upside down.

What does it take to have a successful relationship? Not an easy question probably...! By inverting the question, what does it take to fail a relationship? The following examples can be added when you address it backwards:

- Being violent or abusive
- Unfaithful
- Not providing financially
- Disrespectful

- Untruthful
- Irresponsible
- Ignorant
- Indifferent

By avoiding all the above, a relationship or marriage can work out at least half reasonably by revealing how to prevent a bad one. In other words, on this occasion preventing harm is more important than seeking brilliance. This is because there is too much to lose on the downside than to gain from the upside. Regaining trust after betrayal or disloyalty can be incredibly difficult. This can take considerable amount of time and effort, or it may never be fully restored.

How can I improve my personal finances? This is a question we all probably face at some point in our lives. I've never met anyone who has said, "I have enough savings; I don't need to accumulate more. I want to stop right here and now." However, just because I haven't encountered such a person doesn't mean they don't exist. When faced with these challenging scenarios, there are various approaches we can take. These include finding a job that aligns with your academic qualifications, requesting a promotion or raise within your employment, consider a relocation, or even starting your own business. However, these goals can sometimes represent a challenging task due to various influencing factors such as personal responsibilities, time constraints, associated risks, and, most likely due to safety reasons.

Instead of focusing solely on job-related changes, let's consider a different perspective: how can we effectively reduce our personal finances? For instance, a significant debt can hinder our financial stability. Other common pitfalls include spending more than earning, traveling during peak holiday seasons, using gambling as a distraction, neglecting to track our expenses, purchasing unnecessary expensive items, making late payments, and maintaining luxurious habits that we cannot afford. Well, if these can be prevented our financial situation may happen to be at least in a satisfactory way or we are not filing for bankruptcy any time soon. From time to time, intentionally or not, we encounter various challenges if we want to make a real difference, to push the boundaries of our limits, regardless of our chosen path. There is often a direct correlation between risk and reward. Normally, the higher the risk, the higher the reward. No great ideas, innovation and results are made if we become too rational and reasonable in what we do. This is due to the limitations involved in our reasoning approach. Using an inversion approach does not always solve a problem, but it can provide a clearer understanding and a fresh perspective on how to handle a particular situation.

Over the years, especially when moving homes, we have the tendency to accumulate various items that we don't use or need in the foreseeable future. These items range from clothing to cards, gifts, and more. This accumulation can lead to uncomfortable and unpleasant situations when we try to organise, find, or remove something. Getting rid of those, isn't alway easy, particularly when habits, emotions, or memories are attached to them. However, if a decision is made to remove something which is no longer needed, a helpful approach is: What are the most important items that I want to keep? By focusing on what to retain rather than what to remove, we can find a clearer and more effective solution for decluttering our home. Productivity is another subject that many of us strive for when it comes to a specific time frame. It's also important to flip the question around. "What makes me ineffective and unproductive?" Common factors include setting unrealistic tasks, high usage of distractions and interruptions, jumping between topics without making a real progress, focusing on multitasking, lacking energy, having unclear goals, and frequently postponing deadlines. By avoiding these pitfalls, we can often minimise the risks associated with those and enhance our productivity.

Moreover, generating ideas and to create Xs can represent a challenging task. Sometimes, an easier and more valuable way is to understand how to create non Xs and to avoid them. The inversion technique is not a simple approach that can be easily applied in everyday life. This is largely because we tend to become attached to our ideas, solutions, stories, and beliefs. Once we develop an 'affection' for these concepts, we often find it difficult to put them aside or eliminate them. This process is usually not a priority for us. While it may be well-intentioned, depending on the situation at hand, it can obscure the reality we live in. This occurs for several reasons. Firstly, once we like a decision, shortly after we tend to like that decision even more than the previous occasion. As a result, when we attempt to identify any potential disadvantages or flaws in our ideas, we are hesitant to thoroughly explore them. Secondly, when we hold on to a particular idea or belief and see potential rewards associated with it, we tend to invest our energy in that belief, convinced that the positive outcomes will occur that will lead to the actual benefits. To address this, especially when using the inversion approach, it's important to remove the anticipated incentives.

XVIII
Hope, nothing without it...

In Greek mythology, Prometheus desired to help humankind by stealing fire from the heavens. In response, Zeus, the king of the gods, sought revenge by showing Pandora a box. Pandora was married to Epimetheus, Prometheus's brother. As the first woman created by gods, she was gifted with many beautiful and alluring qualities, including charm and cleverness. Inside the box were numerous unknown evils, problems, and sicknesses that were released in the world. Although she was warned not to open it, her curiosity ended the earthly heaven. Nothing was left behind, but a state of hope.

The meaning behind Pandora's box comes with a handful of descriptions. In this context, the box represents the complications, troubles and misfortunes that life proposes from time to time. Simultaneously, it holds hope, a way of optimism to deal with those problems and challenges for a better future.

What keeps us alive? The relationships we want to cultivate, our ambition in the corporate ladder, the impact that we wish to make in society, our quest for financial comfort, to be able to do things more according to our own desires, to find purpose, to become a parent, a grandparent and to become better in what we do ... All of these would not be possible without hope; to explore life at our full potential, to wake up wittingly and meaningfully each day. Hope, more in a way that displays authenticity and transparency, recognising that difficult challenges are part of journey, allowing some space too, for failure and discomfort.

Hope is sometimes associated to trust, in a way that something will happen in the near future in some way or another. When a future possibility is envisioned, hope can motivate us and strengthen our resilience in pursuing our personal goals. Hope allows us to imagine various scenarios, taking the actions and decisions in the present moment to move closer to those future scenarios. In principle, hope gives us something to look forward to.

XIX
References

Arrien, A. (2011). *Living in gratitude: A journey that will change your life.* Boulder: Sounds True.

Festinger, L. (1957). *A theory of cognitive dissonance.* Stanford: Stanford University Press.

Watkins, A. (2013). *Coherence: The secret science of brilliant leadership.* London: Kogan Page.

Taleb, N.N. (2007). *The Black Swan: The impact of the highly improbable.* New York: Random House.

Marks, H. (2011). *The most important thing: Uncommon sense for the thoughtful investor.* New York: Columbia University Press.

David, S. (2016). *Emotional agility: Get unstuck, embrace change, and thrive in work and life.* New York: Avery.

Maslow, A.H. (1954). *A Theory of Human Motivation.* Psychological Review, 50(4), pp.370-396.

Munger, C. (2005). *Poor Charlie's Almanack, The Essential Wit and Wisdom of Charles T. Munger.* Missouri: Donning Company.

Taleb, N.N. (2001). *Fooled by randomness: The hidden role of chance in life and in the markets.* New York: Texere.

The psychologist Daniel Kahneman... Kahneman, D. (2003). *A perspective on judgement and choice: Mapping bounded rationality.* American Psychologist, 58 (9), 865-878

References

Ekman, P. (1999). *Basic emotions*. In T. Dalgleish and T. Power (Eds). *The Handbook of Cognition and Emotion*. New York: John Wiley & Sons.

Butler, G. and Hope, T. (2018). *Manage Your Mind: The Mental Fitness Guide*. Oxford: Oxford University Press.

Cialdini, R.B. (2006). *Influence: The psychology of persuasion*. Revised ed. New York: Harper Business.

Eurich, T. (2018). *What self-awareness really is and how to cultivate it*. Harvard Business Review. Available at: https://hbr.org/2018/01/what-self-awareness-really-is-and-how-to-cultivate-it [Accessed 17 Dec. 2024].

De Botton, A. (2019). *The School of Life*: An Emotional Education. London: Penguin Books.

De Botton, A. (2004). *Status Anxiety*. London: Hamish Hamilton.

Lyubomirsky, S. (2011). *Pursuing happiness: The architecture of sustainable change*. New York: Wiley.

Fredrickson, B. (1998). *What good are positive emotions?* Review of general Psychology,2(3),300-319.

Tugade, M. Fredrickson, B.L. and Barret, L.F., (2004). Psychological resilience and positive emotional granularity: Examining the benefits of positive emotions on coping and health. *Journal of Personality*, 72(6), 1161-1190.

World Happiness Report, 2023. *World happiness, trust, and social connections in times of crisis*. Available at: https://worldhappiness.report/ed/2023/world-happiness-trust-and-social-connections-in-times-of-crisis/#ranking-of-happiness-2020-2022 [Accessed 17 March. 2023].

Finland and Denmark Happiness, 2021. *The happiest country in the world.* Available at: https://www.youtube.com/watch?v=6Pm0Mn0-jYU [Accessed 11 May. 2021].

World Happiness Report, (2022). *Exploring the biological basis for happiness.* Available at: https://worldhappiness.report / ed /2022/ exploring-the-biological-basis-for-happiness /#:~:text=30%2D40%25%20of%20the%20differences,by%20genetic % 20differences %20between %20people [Accessed 19 Feb. 2022].

Clear, J. (2018). *Atomic habits: An easy & proven way to build good habits & break bad ones.* London: Penguin Books.

Robson, D. (2022). *The expectation effect: How your mindset can transform your life.* London: Canongate Books.

McLaren, K. (2010). *The language of emotions: What your feelings are trying to tell you.* Boulder: Sounds True.

Heuristics, range from reasonable prohibitions...The upside and downside of heuristics as they relate to flexibility are nicely described by Kashdan, T. and Rottenberg, J. (2010). Psychological flexibility as a fundamental aspect of health. *Clinical Psychology review*, 30(7),865-878.

Alexander AG. *The relationship between tobacco smoking calculus and plaque accumulation and gingivitis.* Dental Health (London). 1970;9(1):6–9.

Centre for Disaster Philanthropy, (2023). *Turkey-Syria earthquake.* Available at: https:// disasterphilanthropy .org/ disasters /2023-turkey- syria- earthquake/ (Accessed: [23 Mar.2023].

Smith, J. (1987). *Black Monday.* New York: Financial Press.

Esposito, R.P., Mcadoo, H., & Scher, L. (1976). *The Johari Window as an evaluative instrument for group process Interpersonal Development*, 1975/76, 6, 25-37.

Smith, J. and Doe, A. (2001). 'The Johari Window Test: A Research Note', Journal of Psychology, 15(2), pp. 45-53.

Ware, N. (2021). *Why are we unhappy, the expectation gap*. Available at: https://www.youtube.com/watch?v=9KiUq8i9pbE&t=777s [11 Nov.2021]

Centres for Disease Control and Prevention, (2016). *The relationship between health and happiness*. Available at: https://www.cdc.gov/pcd/issues/2016/16_0309.htm#:~:text =The %20objective %20o f% 20our%20study, physical % 20health% 2C%20and% 20community% 20support [Accessed 24 Dec. 2021].

Scientific American, (2013). *The differences between happiness and meaning in life*. Available at: https://blogs.scientificamerican.com/beautiful-minds/the-differences-between-happiness-and-meaning-in-life/#:~:text=Happiness%20and%20meaning%20are%20strongly,even%20greater%20meaning%20and%20purpose [Accessed 29 Oct. 2022].

To be happy within a given culture depends on...Gruber, J., Mauss, I. and Tamir, (2011). *A dark side of happiness. How, when and why happiness is not good*. Perspectives and psychological studies,6(3),222-233

CNBC, (2023). *85-year Harvard study found the secret to a long, happy, and successful life*. Available at: https://www.cnbc.com/2023/02/10/85-year-harvard-study-found-the-secret-to-a-long-happy-and-successful-life.html [Accessed 03 Aug. 2023]

Aurelius, M. (1862). *The meditations of Marcus Aurelius*. Translated by G. Long. London: George Bell and Sons.

Farnam Street, 2022. *Psychology of Human Misjudgement. Charlie Munger*. Available at: https: //fs.blog /great -talks / psychology-human-misjudgment/ [Accessed 22 Dec. 2022].

Tolle, E., (2001). *Living a life of inner peace*. Novato: New World Library.

Tindale, C.W. (2017). *Oxford guide to effective argument and critical thinking*. Oxford: Oxford University Press.

Singer, M. (2007). The Untethered Soul: *The Journey Beyond Yourself*. Oakland: New Harbinger Publications

Fisher, A. (2004). *The logic of real arguments*. 2nd edn. Cambridge: Cambridge University Press.

Stanford Encyclopaedia of Philosophy, (2024). *Philosophical Argument*. Available at: https: //plato. stanford. edu/ entries/ argument/ [Accessed 23 Jan.2025].

Kwik, J. (2020). Limitless: *Upgrade your brain, learn anything faster, and unlock your exceptional life*. London: Hay House.

HelpGuide, (n.d.). *Dealing with uncertainty*. Available at: https://www.helpguide.org/mental-health/anxiety/dealing-with-uncertainty. Accessed: [09 Feb.2022].

Raizada, M. (2023). *Happy Hormones, Happy You*. Lancashire: Beaten Track

Kübler-Ross, E. (1969). *On death and dying*. New York: Macmillan.

Encyclopaedia of Philosophy, (2024). *Validity and soundness*. Available at: https://iep.utm.edu/val-snd/ [Accessed 29 Jan. 2025].

Porter, E.H. (1913). *Pollyanna*. Boston: The Page Company.

Demartini, J. (2012). *The value factor: The secret to creating an inspired and fulfilling life*. Carlsbad: Hay House.

Study.com, (2024). *Logical argument: definition, parts & examples*. Available at: https://study.com/academy/lesson/logical-argument-definition-parts-examples.html [Accessed19 Dec 2024].

Aurelius, M. (2002). *Meditations. Translated by G. Hays*. New York: Modern Library.

Sokol, B.W. Grouzet, F.M.E., and Muller, U., eds., (2013). *Self-regulation and autonomy: Social and developmental dimensions of human conduct*. Cambridge: Cambridge University Press.

Barrett, L.F. Lewis, M., and Haviland-Jones, J.M., eds. (2016). Handbook of emotions. 4th ed. New York: Guilford Press.

Soni, D. (2019). *An introduction to Johari Window*. Kindle edition.

Breuning, L.G. (2015). *Habits of a happy brain: Retrain your brain to boost your serotonin, dopamine, oxytocin, & endorphin levels*. Dallas: Adams Media.

Brandreth, G. (2013). *The 7 secrets of happiness*. London: Short Books.

National Centre for Biotechnology Information NCBI, (2015). *Genetics of happiness*. Available at: https://pmc.ncbi.nlm.nih.gov/articles/PMC4449495/#:~:text=Results%20of%20studies%20on%20genetic,distributed%20to%20emotion%20and%20mood. [Accessed 15 Jan. 2022].

Haidt, J., (2006). The happiness hypothesis: *Finding modern truth in ancient wisdom*. New York: Basic Books.

University of Pittsburgh Medical Centre, UPMC, (2021). Cognitive distortions: What they are and how to stop them. Available at: https: //share. upmc.com /2021 /05/ cognitive-distortions/#:~:text=Labeling%20and%20mislabeling.,you%20 failed%20the%20math%20test

[Accessed 12 Nov. 2021].

University of Washington, n.d. *The stages of grief: Accepting the unacceptable.* Available at: https://wellbeing.uw.edu/the-stages-of-grief-accepting-the-unacceptable/ [Accessed 17 June. 2021].

De Waal, F. (2009). *The Age of Empathy: Nature's Lessons for a Kinder Society.* Harmony Books, New York.

De Waal, F. (2016). *Are We Smart Enough to Know How Smart Animals Are?* W.W. Norton & Company, New York.

Two Monkeys Were Paid Unequally - *The Pillars of Morality.* [video] YouTube. Available at: https://www.youtube.com/watch?v=meiU6TxysCg [Accessed 27 June 2023].

Kant, I. (2012). *Groundwork of the Metaphysics of Morals.* Translated by M. Gregor. Introduction by C.M. Korsgaard. Cambridge University Press, Cambridge.

Callanan, J. (2013). Kant's Groundwork of the Metaphysics of Morals: An Edinburgh Philosophical Guide. Edinburgh University Press, Edinburgh.

Harvard Health Publishing, (2021). *Feel-good hormones: How they affect your mind, mood, and body.* Available at: https://www.health.harvard.edu/mind-and-mood/feel-good-hormones-how-they-affect-your-mind-mood-and-body [Accessed 11 Dec. 2022].

Healthline, (2022). Stages of grief: *What they are and how to navigate them.* Available at: https://www.healthline.com/health/stages-of-grief [Accessed 03 June. 2021].

O'Connor, M.F. (2022). The grieving brain: *The surprising science of how we learn from love and loss.* New York: HarperOne.

Kessler, D. (2019). *Finding meaning: The sixth stage of grief.* New York: Scribner.

Stanford University, C. (2023). *Validity and soundness of an argument.* Available at: https://web.stanford.edu/~bobonich/terms.concepts/valid.sound.html [Accessed 02 Feb. 2025].

Cyrulnik, B. (2009). *A wonderful misfortune.* London: Other Press.

Centre for Clinical Interventions (CCI), n.d. *Unhelpful thinking styles.* Available at: https://www.cci.health.wa.gov.au/~/media/CCI/Mental-Health- 11--Unhelpful-Thinking-Styles [16 Sep.2021].

Harvard University, 2022. *Identifying negative automatic thought patterns.* Available at: https://sdlab.fas.harvard.edu/cognitive-reappraisal/identifying-negative-automatic-thought-patterns [Accessed 17 March. 2022].

Cambridge University Press, 2021. *Identifying and challenging unhelpful thinking.* Available at: https://www.cambridge.org/core/journals/advances-in-psychiatric-treatment/article/identifying-and-challenging-unhelpful-thinking/6A41268D959EC97545859A9EAA8065B0 [Accessed 10 June. 2021].

Kahneman, D. (2011). *Thinking, fast and slow.* New York: Farrar, Straus and Giroux.

Hayes, N. (2001). *Understanding psychology.* London: Hodder & Stoughton.

Damasio, A. (2021). *Feeling & knowing: Making minds conscious.* London: Pantheon Books.

DeMoss, N.L. (2009). *Choosing gratitude: Your journey to joy.* Chicago: Moody Publishers.

Kwik, J. (2022). *How gratitude rewires the brain.* Available at: https://www.youtube.com/watch?v=eYoocycgMPw&t=454s [Accessed 23 March. 2023].

Plutchik, R, (1991). *Emotion: A psycho-evolutionary synthesis.* New York: Harper & Row.

Computing History, (2024). *ULCC News March 1973 – Newsletter 53. Swing Tree Analogy.* Available at: https://www.computinghistory.org.uk/det/4523/ULCC-News-March-1973-Newsletter-53/ [Accessed 18 Dec. 2024].

Schrauf, R.W. and Müller, N. (2014). *Language development over the lifespan.* New York: Routledge.

Meisner, G.B. (2018). *The golden ratio: The divine beauty of mathematics.* New York: Race Point Publishing.

Rosenberg, J.I. (2019). *90 seconds to a life you love: How to master your difficult feelings to cultivate lasting confidence, resilience, and authenticity.* New York: Little, Brown Spark.

Aesop, (2018). *Aesop's fables: The classic edition.* Illustrated by C. Santore. Philadelphia: Applesauce Press.

Festinger, L. (1957). *A theory of cognitive dissonance.* Stanford: Stanford University Press.

Dobelli, R. (2013). *The art of thinking clearly: Better thinking, better decisions.* London: Sceptre.

Sharma, P. (2022). *The art of clear thinking*: Mental models for better reasoning, judgment, analysis, and learning. Independently published.

Parrish, S. (2019). *The great mental models: General thinking concepts.* Farnham: Farnham Street Media.

Sprouts, (2021). *Confirmation bias*. Available at: https://www.youtube.com/watch?v=Kho5KvPBDSw [Accessed 05 Sep. 2022].

Durmus, M. (2020). *Cognitive biases: A brief overview of over 160*. Independently published.

Ariely, D. (2008). *Predictably irrational: The hidden forces that shape our decisions*. New York: HarperCollins.

Cherry, K. (2023). *What is a confirmation bias?*. Very well Mind. Available at: https://www.verywellmind.com/what-is-a-confirmation-bias-2795024 [Accessed 23 July 2023].

Nickerson, R.S. (1998). Confirmation bias: A ubiquitous phenomenon in many guises. Review of General Psychology, 2(2), pp.175–220.

The Swedish investor, (2022). *Mental models by Charlie Munger*. Available at: https://www.youtube.com/watch?v=cgfuEEnsuAc&list=PLI84Sf0aDgazRojpYTLTXFE6Iaf5bkY r [Accessed 23 July 2022].

Anderson C. A. (1982). *Inoculation and counter explanation: Debiasing techniques in the perseverance of social theories*. Social Cognition, 1, 126–139.

Arkes H. R. Dawes R. M., & Christensen C. (1986). *Factors influencing the use of a decision rule in a probabilistic task*. Organizational Behaviour and Human Decision Processes, 37, 93–110.

Behavioural Insights Team, (2024). *How confirmation bias stops us solving problems*. Available at: https://www.bi.team/blogs/how-confirmation-bias-stops-us-solving-problems/ [Accessed 17 Mar 2024].

Daniel, E. (2022). Dunning-Kruger effect: *Between self-perception and reality*. Independently published.

Dunning, D. and Kruger, J. (2000). The Dunning-Kruger effect. *Journal of Personality and Social Psychology*, 77(6), pp.1121–1134.

National Air and Space Museum, (2023). *Apollo 16*. Available at: https://airandspace.si.edu/explore/stories/apollo-missions/apollo-16#:~:text=Landing%20in%20the%20previously%20unexplored,ultraviolet%20camera%20on%20the%20Moon

[Accessed 19 Jan. 2023].

Bock, M., & Klinger, E. (1986). Interaction of emotion and cognition in word recall. Psychological Research, 48, 99-106.

Bradley, M.M., Greenwald, M.K., Petry, M.C., & Lang, P.J. (1992). Remembering pictures: Pleasure and arousal in memory. Journal of Experimental Psychology: Learning, Memory, and Cognition, 18, 379-390.

Beaton, C., (2016). *The overview effect: How to get unstuck and shake up your professional perspective.* Forbes. Available at: https://www.forbes.com/sites/carolinebeaton/2016/08/24/the-overview-effect-how-to-get-unstuck-and-shake-up-your-professional-perspective/ [Accessed 03 Feb. 2023].

Tindle, H.A. Chang, Y., Kuller, L.H., Manson, J.E., Robinson, J.G., Rosal, M.C., Siegel, G.J., and Matthews, K.A., (2009). *Is the glass half empty or half full? A prospective study of optimism and coronary heart disease in the normative aging study.* Psychosomatic Medicine, 71(8), pp. 839–845.

British Psychological Society, (2023). Replication: *Glass half full, half empty, or irrelevant?* Available at: https://www.bps.org.uk/psychologist/replication-glass-half-full-half-empty-or-irrelevant [Accessed 13 Jun. 2023].

Descartes, R. (1999). *The principles of philosophy. Translated by J. Veitch.* Prometheus Books.

Descartes, R. (2022). *Discourse on the method of rightly conducting one's reason and of seeking truth in the sciences.* Sanage Publishing House LLP.

Hanoch, Y., (2020). When Less Is More: How the Paradox of Choice Shapes Our Decisions. Basic Books.

Sage, Theoretical Psychology. Information, Emotional Arousal and the Ecological Reframing of the Yerkes-Dodson Law https://journals.sagepub.com/doi/10.1177/0959354304044918

Anderson, K.J., Revelle W., & Lynch, M.J. (1994). Caffeine, impulsivity, and memory scanning: A comparison of two explanations for the Yerkes-Dodson effect. Motivation and Emotion, 13, 1-20.

Stanford Encyclopaedia of Philosophy, (2020). *Descartes' Ideas.* Available at: https://plato.stanford.edu/entries/descartes-ideas/
[Accessed 29 Oct. 2023].

GCP Awards, (2016). *8-year-old polyglot Bella Devyatkina can already speak 8 different languages: Child prodigy. Medium.* Available at: https://medium.com/@gcpawards/8-year-old-polyglot-bella-devyatkina-can-already-speak-8-different-languages-child-prodigy-59314ba252b2 [Accessed 19 Mar. 2022].

ScienceDirect, (2022). *Brain waves.* Available at: https://www.sciencedirect.com/topics/agricultural-and-biological-sciences/brain-waves [Accessed 17 March. 2022].

Schnitzler A, Gross J. (2006). *Normal and pathological oscillatory communication in the brain.* Nat Rev Neurosci. 2005; 6:285–296. 10.1038/nrn1650

Oxford Academic, (2023). *Brain article: The role of brain connectivity in neurological disorders.* 147/9/2966/7672954

Muse, (2022). *A deep dive into brainwaves: Brainwave frequencies explained.* Available at: https://choosemuse.com/blogs/news/a-deep-dive-into-brainwaves-brainwave-frequencies-explained-2 [Accessed 19 Mar. 2022]

Clifford, C. (2019). *Stanford study: Working longer hours doesn't make you more productive—here's how to get more done by doing less.* CNBC.

Healium, (2022). *Brainwaves explained.* Available at: https://www.tryhealium.com/2022/08/30/alpha-brainwaves-explained/ [Accessed 30 Mar. 2022].

SAGE Journals, (2018). *Big data analytics and artificial intelligence: The future of decision-making.* Brain state oscillations. 10.26599/BSA.2018.9050008

Wikipedia, (2023). Grigori Perelman. Available at: https://en.wikipedia.org/wiki/Grigori_Perelman

Clay Mathematics Institute, (2008). *Poincaré Conjecture.* Available at: https://www.claymath.org/millennium/poincare-conjecture/ [Accessed 10 July. 2023].

McGovern Institute for Brain Research, (2023). *Do we use only 10 percent of our brain?* Available at: https://mcgovern.mit.edu/2024/01/26/do-we-use-only-10-percent-of-our-brain/#:~:text=In%201907%2C%20William%20James%2C%20a,the%20brain%E2%80%94setting%20this%20common [Accessed 10 Jan. 2023].

Mercedes-Benz Public Archive, n.d. *Benz Velo and Comfortable 1894–1901.* Available at: https://mercedes-benz-publicarchive.com/marsClassic/en/instance/ko/Benz-Velo-and-Comfortable-1894---1901.xhtml?oid=4355 [Accessed 11 Dec. 2023].

The Engineer, n.d. Late great engineers: *Gottlieb Daimler and Wilhelm Maybach*. Available at: https://www.theengineer.co.uk/content/in-depth/late-great-engineers-gottlieb-daimler-automotive-pioneer/ [Accessed 17 Dec. 2023].

Goodwood, n.d. *Taming the land speed record-breaking Blitzen Benz*. Available at: https: //www. goodwood.com /grr/ event-coverage/members-meeting/taming-the-land-speed-record-breaking-blitzen-benz/ [Accessed 12 Jan. 2023].

Volkswagen, n.d. An ode to the Bug. Available at: https://www.vw.com/en/newsroom/lifestyle-and-heritage/an-ode-to-the-bug.html [Accessed 19 Jan. 2024].

Sullivan, R.J. (2008). *An Introduction to Kant's Ethics*. Cambridge University Press, Cambridge.

Schwarz W. Hartman R. (2003). *Immanuel Kant Logic*. Dover Publications, New York.

Surge, M. (2020). *Kant Moral Philosophy*. Available at: https://www.youtube.com/results?search_query=michael+surge+kant [Accessed 28 Dec 2023].

Institute of Physics (IOP), n.d. *The invention of the airbag*. Available at: https://spark.iop.org/invention-air-bag [Accessed 12 Jan. 2024].

ResearchGate, n.d. *Nissan Bluebird noise suppression system*. Available at: https:// www.researchgate.net /figure/ Nissan-bluebird-noise- suppression-system_fig10_327969134 [Accessed 14 Jan. 2024].

Wikiwand, n.d. *Toshiba TLCS*. Available at: https://www.wikiwand.com/en/articles/Toshiba_TLCS [Accessed 23 Mar. 2023].

Bugatti, n.d. Bugatti Speedline: *A Record-Breaking Brand.* Available at: https: //newsroom. bugatti.com / press-releases / bugatti-speedline-a-record-breaking-brand [Accessed 19 May. 2022].

Scientific American, (2023*). Short naps have major benefits for your mind.* Available at: https://www.scientificamerican.com/article/short-naps-have-major-benefits-for-your-mind/ [Accessed 18 Jun. 2023].

Ainsworth M, Lee S, Cunningham M (2012). Rates and rhythms: *A synergistic view of frequency and temporal coding in neuronal networks.* Neuron 75(4): 572–583.

Arnsten A. F. (1998). *The biology of being frazzled.* Science 280 1711–1712 10.1126/science.280.5370.1711

Library of Congress, n.d. Automotive Industry: *A Brief History of the Automotive Industry.* Available at: https://guides.loc.gov/automotive-industry/history [Accessed 25 Apr. 2023].

Sharp Magazine, (2022). *Audi A8: History and Evolution.* Available at: https://sharpmagazine.com/2022/04/06/audi-a8-history-and-evolution/ [Accessed 06 May. 2024].

Audi Media Centre, n.d. *Audi A8 L Innovation.* Available at: https://www.audi-mediacenter.com/en/audi-a8-l-53 [Accessed 11 Jul 2022].

Motor Hive, n.d. *Bugatti Chiron Documentary – National Geographic.* Available at: https://motorhive.co.uk/bugatti-chiron-documentary-national-geographic/ [Accessed 15 Dec. 2021].

WELT Documentary, n.d. *The secrets of luxury sedans: How S-Class, Maybach and EQS are made.* Available at: https://www.youtube.com/watch?v=TWLyRQbvr6o&t=1517s [Accessed 14 Sep. 2021].

Audi, n.d. *What does it take for a car to become an Audi?* [YouTube video]. Available at: https://www.youtube.com/watch?v=m4aNXgl4U9c [Accessed 12 Nov. 2020].

Syed, M. (2020). *The Power of Diverse Thinking*. London: John Murray Press.

TEDx Talks, (2020). *How to Engage Your Team's Cognitive Diversity*. Available at: https://www.youtube.com/watch?v=1HdHf4CoQhI [Accessed 23 Dec. 2023].

Buchanan, T.W., & Lovallo, W.R. (2001). *Enhanced memory for emotional material following stress-level cortisol treatment in humans.* Neuroendocrinology, 26, 307-317.

Christianson, S.A. (1992). *Emotional stress and eyewitness memory*: A critical review. Psychological Bulletin, 112, 284-309.

Akam T, Kullmann DM (2010). *Oscillations and filtering networks support flexible routing of information.* Neuron 67(2): 308–320

McClelland D, Paulsen O (2009). *Neuronal oscillations and the rate-to-phase transform:* Mechanism, model and mutual information. Journal of Physiology 587(Pt 4): 769–785.

SAGE Journals, 2018. *Understanding the Paradox of Choice in Decision Making*, 10.1177/2398212818794827

Bar-Haim Y., Pine D. S., (2013). *Cognitive training research and the search for a transformative, translational, developmental cognitive neuroscience.* Dev. Cogn. Neurosci. 4 1–2 10.1016/j.dcn.2013.02.001

Barrett L. F., Mesquita B., Ochsner K. N., Gross J. J. (2007). *The experience of emotion.* Annu. Rev. Psychol. 58 373 10.1146/annurev.psych.58.110405.085709

Smith, J.R. and Haslam, S.A., (2017). *Social Psychology: Revisiting the Classic Studies.* Illustrated ed. London: SAGE Publications.

Baumeister, R.F. (2007). *Social Psychology and Human Nature.* London: SAGE Publications

Compton, W.C. and Hoffman, E.L. (2019). *Positive Psychology:* The Science of Happiness and Flourishing. 3rd ed. London: SAGE Publications.

Reference List: Hanson, R. (2014). *Hardwiring Happiness: How to reshape your brain and your life.* Paperback ed. London: Rider.

Zen Tao, (2024). *Tree swing project management*: Available at: https://www.zentao.pm/blog/tree-swing-project-management-tire-analogy-426.html [Accessed 12 Sep 2023].

Business Balls, (2024). *Tree swing cartoon pictures – early versions.* Available at: https://www.businessballs.com/amusement-stress-relief/tree-swing-cartoon-pictures-early-versions/ [Accessed 03 Jan. 2025].

Brandreth, G. (2024). *The 7 Secrets of Happiness*: An Optimist's Journey. Hardcover ed. London: Short Books

CNBC, (2019). Stanford study: *Longer hours don't make you more productive* — here's how to get more done by doing less. Available at: https://www.cnbc.com/2019/03/20/stanford-study-longer-hours-doesnt-make-you-more-productive-heres-how-to-get-more-done-by-doingless.html#:~:text=In%20his%20research%2C%20economics%20professor%20John%20Pencavel%20found,putting%20in%20any%20more%20hours%20would%20be%20pointless. [Accessed 02 Dec. 2023].

Denes, G. (2023). *The Psychology of Lying and Misrepresentations:* Behavioural, Neuroscientific and Neuropsychological Perspectives. Oxford: Routledge.

Ryan, R.M. and Deci, E.L. (2018). *Self-Determination Theory: Basic Psychological Needs in Motivation, Development, and Wellness.* New York: Guilford Press.

Gilovich, T. (1990). *Differential construal and the false consensus effect.* Journal of Personality and Social Psychology, 59, 623–634.

Frijda Nico. *On the Nature and Function of Pleasure.* In: Kringelbach ML, Berridge KC, editors. Pleasures of the Brain. New York: Oxford University Press; 2010. pp. 99–112.

Kesebir P, Diener E. *In Pursuit of Happiness*: Empirical Answers to Philosophical Questions. Perspectives on Psychological Science. 2008;3:117–25. doi: 10.1111/j.1745-6916.2008.00069.x.

Griffin D. W., Dunning D., Ross L. (1990). *The role of construal processes in overconfident prediction and judgment.* Journal of Personality and Social Psychology, 59, 1128–1139.

Concepts Unwrapped, 2019. *Fundamental Attribution Error* [video] YouTube. Available at: https://www.youtube.com/watch?v=AdrDAik86rc [Accessed 10 December 2022].

Eurich, T. (2018). *What Self-Awareness Really Is and How to Cultivate It.* Harvard Business Review. Available at: https://hbr.org/2018/01/what-self-awareness-really-is-and-how-to-cultivate-it [Accessed 30 Jan 2024].

Kant, I. (2007). *Critique of Pure Reason.* Translated by M. Weigelt. Penguin Classics, London.

Positive Psychology, (2021). *Fundamental Attribution Error.* Available at: https: //positivepsychology.com / fundamental-attribution-error/ [Accessed 05 Feb. 2022].

Davidson RJ, Irwin W. *The Functional Neuroanatomy of Emotion and Affective Style*. Trends in Cognitive Sciences. 1999;3(1):11–21. doi: 10.1016/s1364-6613(98)01265-0.

Fredrickson BL, et al. *Open Hearts Build Lives*: Positive Emotions, induced through Loving-Kindness Meditation, Build Consequential Personal Resources. Journal of Personality and Social Psychology. 2008;95(5):1045–62. doi: 10.1037/a0013262.

Berlin, I. (2002). *Notes on prejudice*. In Silvers R. B., Epstein B. (Eds.), Striking terror: (pp. 31–38). New York, NY: New York Review of Books.

The Decision Lab, (2018). *Fundamental Attribution Error*. Available at: https://thedecisionlab.com/biases/fundamental-attribution-error
[Accessed 30 Jan 2022].

Borgida E., Nisbett R. E. (1977). *The differential impact of abstract vs concrete information on decisions*. Journal of Applied Social Psychology, 7, 258–271.

Farnam S, (2022). *Kantian Fairness Tendency*. Available at: https://fs.blog/kantian-fairness-tendency/ [Accessed 22 Jun 2022].

Liu, C. (2018). *Don't Underestimate the Power of Luck When It Comes to Success in Business*. Harvard Business Review. Available at: <https:// hbr.org/ 2021/06/ dont-underestimate -the-power-of-luck-when-it-comes-to-success-in-business> [Accessed 13 December 2023].

Sher, G. (2024). *Four Kantian Fairness*. In: Oxford Scholarship Online. Oxford University Press.

BBC, (2022). *What makes some people luckier than others?* Available at: https:// www.bbc.co.uk/ videos/ c9e9lvd3x09o [Accessed 30 December 2024].

Christensen, C.M., Hall, T., Dillon, K., and Duncan, D.S. (2016). *Competing Against Luck: The Story of Innovation and Customer Choice*. Harper Business, New York.

Frank, R.H. (2016). Success and Luck: *Good Fortune and the Myth of Meritocracy*. Princeton University Press, Princeton.

Veritasium, (2019). *Is Success Luck or Hard Work?* Available at: https://www.youtube.com/watch?v=3LopI4YeC4I [Accessed 19 Jan 2021].

Wilson, M.E. (2019). *Antibiotics: What Everyone Needs to Know®*. Oxford University Press, Oxford.

NHS, (2023). *Antibiotic and Antimicrobial Resistance*. Available at: https://www.nhs.uk/conditions/antibiotics/antibiotic-antimicrobial-resistance/#:~:text=many%20infections%20are%20caused%20by,for%20treating%20more%20serious%20conditions [Accessed 09 Nov. 2023].

Bryc, W. (1995). The normal distribution: Characterizations with applications. Springer-Verlag.

Stats Channel, (2022). *Standard Normal Distribution Tables, Z Scores, Probability & Empirical Rule – Stats*. Available: https://www.youtube.com/watch?v=CjF_yQ2N638.

Chhikara, R. (1989). *The inverse Gaussian distribution:* Theory, methodology, and applications. New York: Marcel Dekker.

NPR, (2015). *Men are obese in America, and gap is widening*. Available at: https:// www.npr.org/ sections/thesalt/ 2015/ 11/ 13/ 455883665

Gitlow, H. (2009). *Lean Six Sigma for green belts*. Upper Saddle River, NJ: Pearson Education.

U.S. Department of Health and Human Services, (2004). *The health consequences of smoking: A report of the Surgeon General. Atlanta*, GA: U.S. Department of Health and Human Services, Centres for Disease Control and Prevention, National Centre for

Chronic Disease Prevention and Health Promotion, Office on Smoking and Health.

Mathur, A. (2021). *The uncomfortable truth*. London: Hachette UK.

Top Gear, (2022). *Wolfgang Dürheimer: The man who changed the world*. Available at: https://www.topgear.com/car-news/insider/wolfgang-durheimer-man-who-changed-world.Accessed: [27 Feb. 2002].

Learnlife. (2023). *The neuroscience of unlearning*. Available at: https://blog.learnlife.com/the-neuroscience-of-unlearning. Accessed: [02 Sep.2022].

Church Life Journal, (2020) *Unlearning is the new learning*. A neuroscientific and theological case for how and why to see the world differently. Available at: https://churchlifejournal.nd.edu/articles/unlearning-is-the-new-learning-a-neuroscientific-and-theological-case-for-how-and-why-to-see-the-world-differently/ Accessed: [29 Jun 2021].

Smith, J. (2023). *Understanding modern sociology', Sociological Research*, 21(3), pp. 45–67. DOI: 10.1177/14782103231176605.

Baldacchino, J. (2013). *Willed forgetfulness: the arts, education and the case for unlearning*. Studies in Philosophy and Education 32(4): 415–430.

Biesta, G., (2009). *Good education in an age of measurement: on the need to reconnect with the question of purpose in education*. Educational Assessment, Evaluation and Accountability 21(1): 33–46.

Chokr, NN. (2009). *Unlearning: Or How Not to Be Governed?* Exeter: Imprint Academic.

Contu, A., Grey C., Örtenblad, A. (2003). Against learning. Human Relations 56(8): 931–95

Hsu, SW., (2021). *Exploring an alternative: Foucault-Chokr's unlearning approach to management education.* The International Journal of Management Education 19(2): 100496.

BBC News, (2013). *A Point of View: Why people sometimes prefer lies to the truth.* Available at: https://www.bbc.co.uk/news/magazine-24077633. Accessed: [22 Jul.2023].

Webb, J. (2022). *Beware brutal honesty: It may be a sign of a toxic person.* Psychology Today. Available at: https://www.psychologytoday.com/gb/blog/childhood-emotional-neglect/202211/beware-brutal-honesty-it-may-be-sign-toxic-person. Accessed: [28 Sep 2022].

Cherry, K. (2021). *Is it ever okay to lie? Verywell Mind.* Available at: https://www.verywellmind.com/is-it-ever-okay-to-lie-5118228.
Accessed: [02 Mar.2021].

Smith, J. (2023). *Remembering the wisdom of Charlie Munger. Forbes.* Available at: https://example.com. (Accessed: 2 January 2024).

Clear, J. (2019). *Inversion: The crucial thinking skill nobody ever taught you.* Available at: https://jamesclear.com/inversion. Accessed: [23 Dec. 2021].

CNBC, (2018). Charlie Munger: The Power of not making stupid decisions. Available at https://www.cnbc.com/2017/08/04/charlie-munger-the-power-of-not-making-stupid-decisions.html

Impey, R. and Bailey, P. (2021). *Pandora's box: A Bloomsbury reader.* Brown book band: Bloomsbury Publishing.

Harrison, J. (2013). *Pandora's Box', Journal of Hellenic Studies, Volume (Issue), pp.* Pages. Available at: https://www.cambridge.

org/core/journals/journal-of-hellenic-studies/article/abs/pandoras-box/3A8FA44FCC3806F6B5192A94F8E0485D

Wikipedia, (n.d.). *Pandora's box*. Available at: https://en.wikipedia.org/wiki/Pandora%27s_box. Accessed: [06 Jan.2021].

Seligman, M.E.P. (2018). *The hope circuit: A psychologist's journey from helplessness to optimism.* New York: Public Affairs.

Argyris, C. (1992). *Theory in practice: increasing professional effectiveness.* San Francisco: Jossey-Bass.

Clay D. L., Anderson W. P., & Dixon W. A. (1993). *Relationship between anger expression and stress in predicting depression.* Journal of Counselling and Development, 2, 91–94.

Cohen, S., Kamarck, T., & Mermelstein, R. (1983). *A global measure of perceived stress.* Journal of Health and Social Behaviour, 2, 386–396.

Egéa-Kuehne, D. (2008). *Levinas and education: at the intersection of faith and reason.* New York: Routledge.

www.ingramcontent.com/pod-product-compliance
Lightning Source LLC
Chambersburg PA
CBHW030314080526
44584CB00012B/573